MEANING IN CRAFTS

MEANING IN CRAFTS

Edward L. Mattil

The Pennsylvania State University

Englewood Cliffs, N. J.

PRENTICE-HALL, INC.

1959

Maryland Institute

BALTIMORE, MD.

PREFACE

THIS BOOK was written for adults who work with children or who plan to work with children. It is a book of craft ideas intended to help to develop good crafts programs based upon an understanding of the meaning of crafts in elementary education. It is important to differentiate between the "making of things," and crafts which help with the creative, social, emotional, physical, and aesthetic growth of children. Products result from each approach, but only from the latter can one expect products which are a record of a meaningful experience.

Whatever reason one may have for considering the inclusion of arts and crafts activities in elementary education, the question of the value of these activities is certain to arise. Those who have made arts and crafts an integral part of education and allowed them to become part of the very fabric of daily living need no reassuring as to the values. They are self-evident.

Today, as in no other time in our history, the importance of creative thinking is uppermost in the minds of leaders in all walks of life. It is important to master skills and to acquire information, but more important is the use of such skills and information for creative living. There is a hypothesis which suggests that only after one has mastered skills and techniques and acquired basic knowledge can the process of creating begin. This hypothesis is challenged by those who contend that creating is a way of uninhibited, unblocked thinking, a kind of thinking which has no limitations and which is open to discovery, exploration, and invention. This is an attitude to foster in childhood. It will unfold while the individual acquires some skills and information in adolescence. And it will be free to blossom and bear fruit in adulthood. This attitude or way of working is not limited to the arts, but rather is fostered by the arts for the continuance and development in every endeavor.

It becomes clear, then, that to support the latter theory does in no way suggest that the arts in education are an end in themselves, that they are permissive or uncontrolled, or that they reject the learning of techniques and information. It does suggest, however, that elementary school arts and crafts are not product centered, but are concerned with the fullest development of the individual, with the product resulting as an outgrowth of his development.

The arts and crafts present an opportunity for the creative development of the elementary child, a means of enriching learning situations, a catalyst for the integration of information, a way of developing individual sensitivity and appreciation, and finally a means of bringing genuine joy and satisfaction into the lives of children.

The author wishes to acknowledge the great help and inspiration of his wife, Polly, and his son, Michael. He is especially indebted to Dr. Viktor Lowenfeld for his constant encouragement and wisdom and to the entire staff of the Department of Art Education at The Pennsylvania State University, where work is truly an inspiration. He is indebted also to many wonderful children, who, with their creative efforts, are pictured herein, and to Dr. D. Kenneth Winebrenner, Dr. Louis Hoover, G. E. Von Rosen, Ruth Whorl, Dr. Leon L. Winslow, Elizabeth Stein, Hilda G. Rosenberg, Mary Adeline McKibbin, Helen Copley Gordon, Vera T. Mathes, Pat T. Cravey, Helen Ames, Lillie B. Adams, Pauli Tolman, Dr. John Lembach, Grace Chadwick, Mary Godfrey, Yar G. Chomicky, Elizabeth Yeager, Norma Molinari, and Marilyn Pappas for assistance in lending class work or photographs or granting permission to use photographs. Thanks, too, to many friends who desired to help but who were unable to provide photographs.

Finally, the author wishes to acknowledge his debt to Ed Leos, whose photography is shown many places throughout the book.

EDWARD L. MATTIL

CONTENTS

MEANING

IN CRAFTS TEACHING

1

OUR LANGUAGE is full of words which have a number of meanings thus creating many problems in clear communication. When we speak of art it may be that we think of a single item or it may be that we are thinking of the creative experience of an adult or of a child. It may, in fact, be the whole process that is being considered. It should be clear, however, that what we think of as art for the child cannot be thought of in the same way as art for the artist. There would be less misunderstanding if another term, such as *creative activity,* replaced the term *art* for the works of children. In the same way that art has a multitude of meanings, the word crafts has many different meanings; in fact it has almost as many definitions as definers. There is no doubt about the relatedness of crafts in the varied meanings given to the word or of the relatedness of crafts to craftsmanship. In this book crafts is thought of as a process of creative activities for children in which a product is the result or record of the creative experience.

When we attempt to trace the historical development of crafts, we discover that we become engaged in the examination of almost any piece of hand workmanship which might have any claim to beauty, or for that matter almost any piece of hand work to which decoration has been applied. If, in such a study, we should be privileged to visit a native potter in India working at his primitive wheel, we might ask him, "Why did you become an artist?" To this he might reply, "But I am not an artist, I am a potter, my father was a potter, as was my grandfather, in fact my family have always been potters. We are even called Potter." Curiously we may ask, "But isn't pottery art?" To this the potter may return, "No, it is my livelihood, my industry!" Yet by our concepts of art and crafts this potter may well be an artist as well as a craftsman engaging in his little industry, for as Herbert Read says, "The man who makes becomes potentially, or partially, an artist the moment the things he makes express or excite feelings."

We must assume that the first tools and utensils of primitive man were restricted to the considerations of utility. As the efficiency of the tools or utensils improved there was a steady evolution of form. There came a point in man's development when the matter of choice entered into the picture. He became able to create a variety of clay bowls, each equally efficient at holding grain or water. It was here, then, that he engaged in the process of aesthetic judgment. Since efficiency was not the factor then being considered there had to be another factor at work, the factor of choice or aesthetic judgment.

This very same problem is basic in the crafts which we must consider in elementary education.

Crafts serve as a wholesome outlet for the many fantasies that come into the young child's mind. (Courtesy Junior Art Gallery, Inc., Louisville, Ky.)

We are able in crafts and art education to teach procedures, and every child can learn procedures. However, it is while the procedures are being carried out that the child engages in constant choices or judgments. He may decide why one shape is "better" than another or he may intuitively select or eliminate to arrive at the "better" choice. This selection or choice in which he constantly engages is aesthetic judgment. It surely can be assumed that this aesthetic judgment cannot be developed without activities which call upon the constant use of these qualities which are basically the ones which distinguish man.

It is at this very point where there are many disagreements regarding the teaching of arts and crafts, for many teachers are unable to distinguish between procedures and technique. Procedures are the various activities which can be explained within the general framework of the project which is being introduced. Technique, on the other hand, is the highly individualized use of the materials involved. His technique, then, becomes the child's personal "language" or "handwriting" with materials. It is impossible to teach technique for it simply must grow out of the child's need to express himself. The teacher who believes that technique is something which can be taught may well be only imposing his own technique on the child. Impositions will ultimately become handicaps. It is safe then to say that one can teach procedures and may only help the child to develop his own technique and that aesthetic judgment can only develop when the child has the freedom to make choices in his work.

Our schools cannot limit the teaching of crafts to only a few processes of the artist-craftsman. The constant development of new materials in every industry suggests an ever widening area in crafts. Surely the crafts of clay, wood, weaving, stitchery and many others of the "old standards" will continually hold their place in importance, but it is necessary not to become so bound by traditional materials that one excludes the many exciting possibilities of experimentation with new materials and new processes. It is, however, very easy to become lost in the jungle of gimmicks and gadgets and to conduct a crafts program without depth or meaning. This usually becomes what is commonly called the "product centered program."

In the same way that our schools cannot limit the teaching of crafts to a few processes, they cannot limit the teaching of crafts to a few children. Children may be likened to a handful of seeds from many flowers. At first they may seem more similar than different in many respects. Place these seeds in the earth and nourish them. As they grow and mature their differences become marked. Some remain small and delicate while others are large and brilliant, some bloom early and some late. One thing they may have in common: under good conditions, they all bloom and have their own beauty. Our classrooms are the earth for these seeds, and when fertile and rich bring forth the best. But the classroom can also have the stultifying effect of poor soil in which nothing can grow. This good soil-poor soil analogy can also be applied to the kind of motivations which are used to introduce various crafts. The child may be given the best kind of instruction in procedures and may use the best materials, but if he has nothing to express through the process it becomes a meaningless, mechanical experience. In crafts the child is able to organize his thoughts, ideas, feelings, actions, techniques into a product. If the experience or motivation is shallow, the ideas vague, the feelings disfuse or absent, the resultant product will reflect it. In other words, the product is the record of the complete process.

With the very young child the process exceeds the product in importance. For example, the five or six year old child may, day after day, pound out balls of clay or coils of clay finally joining them into very simple figure concepts. This daily repetition is of prime importance for it is only through this continued repetition that the child gains the sureness or certainty of achievement that is necessary for growth of confidence. One then must paint to learn to paint or pound to learn to pound, or assemble to learn to assemble. In these early efforts, which are significant to growth, the teacher is unwise to place undue emphasis upon the products as such. Rather, the emphasis should be placed upon continued good experiences with materials and a continued involvement in the process.

The problem of process vs. product is a constant topic for discussion, yet it is a reasonably easy concept to grasp. Both the process and the product are of im-

The best motivations are based upon intense personal experiences.

Children who learn to think and work independently can use their free time for constructive activities.
(Courtesy Dorothy Smith, Kewanee, Ill.)

portance in creative craft activities. However, in the earliest years, when the child's ideas come rapidly and do not remain for long, when interest spans are short, motor skill limited, the emphasis is more upon the process of creating. The product during this early phase is important as the record of the child's involvement, his growth, and his level of development. We may be sure that occasionally we find a veritable gem of child art which we wish to preserve, such as a ceramic figure. However, we err when we start with the intention of firing all the work of a kindergarten class for here we focus more upon the product than we do upon the child and his experience in creating a product. As the child grows older it is only natural that the product continually gains in importance until as adults it is no longer possible to do creative work if there are no products to give personal satisfaction. Adults simply can not be satisfied by only engaging in the process phase.

In early childhood when imagination is unfettered, crafts serve as a wholesome outlet for the many fantasies that come into the young mind. Every new thing ever created resulted from the imaginative ability of someone who could imagine or dream beyond the realities of his known world. Leonardo must have been a constant imaginer or dreamer. Children need to have the time to wonder, ponder and dream, and to have a positive outlet for their imaginations. It is just as important that the child develop his powers of imagination as it is for him to develop in social or group activities. It is important for teachers to foster in children the attitude of expecting and liking to work out their own problems instead of yielding to others who may try to force them into accepting ready-made solutions. At the same time they must be shown the need of being able to work with

4

others toward common goals, and to not be so self centered as to be unable to accept criticism and weigh the ideas of others.

All of us want to see children grow to express themselves clearly and to have something to express. If we recall the number of misses Johnny made before he learned to coordinate sufficiently to catch a thrown ball, we will have some idea of the struggle each child has to develop a personal concept in art or crafts. It is only through this struggle with himself that the child truly grows. Think of the child whose parents never let him struggle, rather constantly make every decision for him. When finally on his own and forced to make a decision or a choice he is unable to do so. Crafts teaching then becomes not only the teaching of procedures but also of creating problems which call for personal solutions. How often we have seen the teacher who has the ready-made solution for art or crafts in the form of hectograph patterns. She carefully directs the group of children through every step, selecting and deciding for them, only to arrive with thirty identical products which are as unchildlike as they are uncreative. Such activities not only destroy the opportunity for growth through art experiences but may even affect the child's confidence in his own ability to create.

What then are the basic considerations for the classroom teacher who wishes to use craft activities as an important part of the educational program of children?

Craft Activities Are Creative Activities

All children possess a creative instinct. Sound education provides the climate for the fullest development of this instinct. In crafts, each project must allow the child to think originally and to learn to work independently. Creative children work freely and flexibly, that is they attack each problem without the fear of failure. Such freedom must be carefully preserved. The teacher who begins her teaching with dogma, rules, techniques or patterns will certainly be placing stumbling blocks which can easily destroy the urge and the ability to create. The preservation and fostering of creative thinking and working in children should be the most important goal of education—not just of art education.

Simple materials combined with a variety of scrap items can form the basis for starting a crafts program.

There Are Wide Opportunities for Growth Through Crafts

Education has always considered intellectual development as one of its main objectives. More recently we have come to consider other areas of growth as equally important. Children need to grow proportionately creatively, socially, physically, emotionally and aesthetically. Each of these areas of growth should be evidenced in a crafts program which is truly planned to meet the needs of children.

Creative growth may be seen in the originality of ideas while social growth may be seen in the child's increasing ability to work cooperatively in his group and through evidence of increasing social responsibility with a greater feeling for the needs and feelings of others. Physical growth is easily identified through increasing motor control and the child's ability to coordinate mind-eye and hand. Emotional growth is recognized in the child's ability to identify with his own work. This is the ability to express personal feeling or experiences without a dependency upon stereotypes or cliches. The aesthetic growth of the child appears with an increasing sensitivity to the organization of ideas and feelings by means of the materials, form, color and texture. Where aesthetic growth is not present the child is unable to integrate his thinking, feeling and perceiving into a harmonious organization.

The more the classroom teacher is aware of these many facets of growth, the more able she is to provide a crafts program with meaning. In the program with meaning, crafts become a means of education and not an end in itself.

Crafts Activities Should Provide Opportunities for Problem Solving

Each craft project which is presented should have only enough direction or procedure to assure some measure of success for even the slowest student. It must always have an "open end" which provides the condition for the child to discover things for himself and that the child may have full opportunity to develop his own techniques and express himself in an individual manner.

Craft Teaching Is Not a Passive Role

We tend to be highly critical of the teacher who simply will not allow the child to think for himself. This teacher gives specific directions or patterns which must be followed without deviation. Such teaching is deadly but the antithesis of this kind of teaching is also of little value. The teacher who only hands out materials then leaves the children to "create" out of a vacuum is surely not fulfilling her role as a teacher. The teacher's role is one of establishing a wholesome climate for creative work, providing good motivations, introducing sufficient orderly procedure to insure good basic foundations on which to work and then permitting the child to use his own ideas for the development of his proj-

Group projects should permit individual
interpretations even though directed
toward a common goal.

ect. The teacher should allow the child to work independently until he reaches his own stopping point then try by conversation to stimulate the child's thinking or by activating his passive knowledge so that he is able to go on to a new level of attainment which he would not have otherwise achieved. In effect this means that the teacher cannot be satisfied with everything or anything that the child produces. Rather she strives to see that the child continually raises his level of achievement and develops in himself a desire to do this. Naturally the range of achievement levels is wide in every group so the teacher is forced to use a different set of values for each child.

Craft Teaching Cannot Be Standardized

We speak so often of the individual differences of children but seldom think of the individual differences in teachers or in schools. Each teacher and each school has it's own peculiar set of problems and of opportunities which affect the crafts program. Sometimes quantity or quality of materials may be the determining factor or sometimes it may be the teachers own special areas of interest. Whatever the reasons may be, there is no school too poor nor any teacher so inadequate to excuse the absence of art education in the school program. The arts and crafts program provides one of the very few opportunities for a complete or total educational experience. A total experience is where the child starts with an idea and is able to bring that idea into a tangible form. To begin the teacher needs only the desire for a worthwhile program and the barest amount of materials. Often these materials can be scrap if there is no other source. Given the opportunity, the child will supply the ideas and develop his own techniques. It is reasonable to expect that the more one tries the more proficient one can become as a crafts teacher. Therefore, it is important to begin immediately and to try to grow in the same way which we might expect each child to grow.

MODELING

AND SCULPTURING

2

NO ART program would ever be complete without providing some opportunities to work in three dimensional activities such as modeling and sculpturing. It is one thing to draw or to paint one's experiences on a flat surface but it is a far different experience to create in a three dimensional manner. It is common to find a child who has great difficulty in thinking two dimensionally finding himself quickly and easily when working in a three dimensional material. The teacher may watch a child struggle indefinitely trying to draw a figure with legs crossed but who might immediately solve this problem when working in clay simply by lifting one leg and crossing it over the other. To work in new and different materials can be stimulating in itself and the limitations imposed by each new material causes the child to develop new and different concepts, to vary his mode of expression, experimenting and inventing as he goes. The three dimensional experience can provide opportunities for the child who is more interested in feeling or tactile sensations than he is in seeing or visual sensations.

Non-hardening Modeling Clay

Probably the most widely used of the three dimensional materials is the non-hardening type of clay known generally as plasticene or plastilene. This clay usually contains oil and glycerine which keeps it from hardening permanently. It is considerably less suggestive and not so responsive as earth clays. This plastic modeling clay is popular because it is economical as a result of reuse. It can play an important role especially in the lower elementary grades where the product is not of great importance to the child as compared with the process of creating it. In these lower grades where the children form very small attachments for their products it is perfectly permissible for the teacher to reform the children's products into lumps and reuse it over and over again. However, this should never be done in the presence of the pupils, and only after they have lost interest in what they have done. In working with clay with younger elementary children it is important that the teacher realize that there is no one "right" way of clay modeling. For the older pottery or sculpture student this might not be true, especially if products were to be fired, but with small children the opportunity to develop their own personal techniques is desirable. Unfortunately, many of our art school trained teachers were taught that the only right way to work with clay is to pull the features out of the whole— that is to start with the solid lump of clay pulling or drawing out the ears, nose, pressing out the lips, eyebrows, etc. While this is an entirely satisfactory method of working for some children it is entirely contrary to the natural method used by others. Some children prefer to make each part separately, and put the parts together.

Modeling in plasticene gave this child the opportunity to relive a happy experience. He is eating a hot dog by a wood fire beneath the spreading branches of a large tree. As he worked he made each log, then carefully arranged them for the fire; made each hot dog, then a bun to hold the one he eats. Bit by bit he recreated in his mind and in his modeling his entire experience.

Since we stress the importance of being individuals, we ought to recognize the fact that each individual has his own way of working and can develop a technique only through his work. There is a mistaken notion held by some teachers that, given the materials, the child will create freely by himself. While this is a beautiful thought, unfortunately it is not often true. In most cases it is up to the teacher to provide adequate stimulation or motivation based upon the child's own experiences. Stimulations provided for working in clay with young children are not unlike the stimulations provided for drawing and painting. "I am catching a ball," "I am eating corn on the cob," "I am taking a nap after lunch," "I am petting my cat," are typical of the sort of stimulations which are desirable while working in clay or plasticene. Since this plastic modeling clay is soft and pliable it requires no special tools or equipment. Children can work on the top of a piece of newspaper or old cardboard. This clay keeps best if stored in an air-tight container such as a gallon jar. If the clay becomes old and hard it sometimes can be resoftened by warming it and working glycerine into it.

Common Earth Clay

A second type of clay which is often used in schools is common earth clay. This can be purchased as dry powder to be mixed with water, or it can be purchased in a moist ready-to-use condition. This type of clay can be fired in a kiln if a kiln is available, but as a rule pieces made with this type of clay are permitted to harden by drying in air. Pieces can be softened by soaking them in water. This clay is about the same as the clay which the children might find in a clay bank near the school or along the edge of a stream, except that when purchased it is always in a refined state free of gravel and pebbles. Sometimes it contains certain materials to make it harden more permanently. Earth clay offers definite limitations to the classroom teacher in that it always shrinks during the drying process, preventing the use of any type of framework or armature inside the clay figures. Since a wire armature would not shrink and the clay does, the dry figure is generally broken into many pieces. Therefore, it is essential

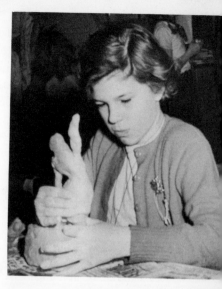

As the child manipulates her clay she develops
a greater sensitivity to the material.

that the teacher working with ordinary clay limit the sort of modeling which the child does to rather compact, bulky figures without delicate appendages. However, such limitations are frequently desirable as they place before each child a new problem requiring a new solution.

If a kiln is available it might be desirable to fire the works of the older children, but it is generally unwise to fire the works of the very young. To fire a product of a child who is doing little more than scribbling in clay is to place undue emphasis upon the product. When using earth clay with a very young child it is permissible to allow them to paint their finished figures if they so desire. Teachers have no business developing "purist" attitudes about the art work of children for any means which fosters sincere, self expression is desirable. Therefore, the painting of clay figures which might be shunned by some adults is acceptable with children.

If the teacher is working with flour clay for the first time, she would do well to mix her clay with small amounts of water until she has mixed it to a good consistency. A good consistency allows the clay to be manipulated without cracking and yet dry or stiff enough so that it doesn't stick much to the hands.

Modeling should be based upon the child's imagination or experiences in the same way as drawing or painting. These solid, compact figures are by ten year old children who show what they wish to be when grown up. One wishes to be a cowboy while the other imagines herself as a mother.

11

A very pleasant and clean way to mix the clay is to put about a pound of flour clay in a plastic bag, add a small amount of water, press out all the air, fasten the bag with a heavy rubber band and give it to one of the children to knead. The kneading experience alone is often very pleasant to young children since it may satisfy a kinesthetic desire. If the clay seems too dry, add a bit more water, or if too moist, add some more clay flour. The teacher will soon discover her own formula for mixing clay and water to come out with a good consistency regularly. The clay will work best if allowed to age for several days before using it after it has been kneaded. It can be stored for an extended period of time in the bag in which it was kneaded.

Into the Kitchen

There is an excellent substitute for clay and plasticene which every teacher can make in her own kitchen or can easily have made by the mothers of the boys and girls in her class. This material could be called a salt ceramic. It is made by using one cup of table salt, one-half cup of corn starch, and three-quarters cup of cold water. These materials are mixed together in the top part of a double boiler and the whole boiler placed over heat. The mixture is stirred constantly and in about two to three minutes it becomes so thick the whole mixture follows the spoon in the stirring process. It quickly reaches a consistency similar to bread dough, and when it does it is dumped on to a piece of wax paper or aluminum foil and allowed to cool. When it has cooled sufficiently to be handled it is kneaded with the hands for several minutes after which it is ready for use. It can be stored away for several days if wrapped in wax paper until ready to be used. Salt ceramic will harden to a consistency of stone and makes excellent material to paint with any type of paint. Salt ceramic has many classroom advantages over clay. It does not shrink when drying and, therefore, permits the use of any type of armature. For example, if a child is making a dog and needs to strengthen the legs, wire pipe cleaners or tooth picks inserted into the legs to strengthen them will work satisfactorily, since there will be no shrinkage. Because it dries very hard it has a much greater durability than the ordinary earth clay which remains unfired. Perhaps the one feature which teachers like the most is its cleanliness. When this gets on the floors of the classroom it does not powder and get dust all over the school.

Through the use of the armature a greater variety of figures can be created with the salt ceramic. If the children have seen a circus, or have been to the zoo or have even seen a movie showing many types of wild animals, they might wish to create animals from salt. It would be quite difficult to make animals like a giraffe with its extremely long neck or the gorilla with its large upstretched arms if the child were unable to use an armature. Using material of this sort often suggests group projects in which each child's product plays a part. This might be called group modeling. To use a circus as an example, with each child modeling

12

the part which interested him most or perhaps to do a Christmas scene in which each child selects one of the major or minor figures to model. This sort of activity is especially good when children are in the ten to twelve year old group for here the meaning of cooperation can be objectively taught. When the child sees a completed group modeling, he carries away a feeling of satisfaction for the completed project fully realizing what the group did as a whole he never could have done himself.

The ease in handling the salt ceramic lends itself to many other interesting projects such as the creation of Christmas ornaments. With small children this could be done simply by rolling balls of different sizes and shapes around a knotted string. These could be painted and decorated in whatever manner the children desire. If the teacher prefers, the whole salt mass can be colored while it is being made simply by adding a few drops of vegetable dye. The salt in the mixture seems to make the color more brilliant and luminous. The children can roll small balls of different sizes and shapes and put holes into them with a match stick, paint them with brilliant colors and string them and have the most interesting beads for their make-believe costumes and these can be shellaced if they desire. Christmas decorations can be made for the tree by patting some flat, like cookie dough, and cutting out shapes of animals or birds or geometric shapes. They can put a hole into these with a match stick and put them away to dry. Later these could be painted and finally decorated with metalic paints and used for Christmas tree ornaments. A little bit of metalic paint is always exciting for children in decorating.

Wire Sculpture

Sculpturing need not be limited to solid forms but can sometimes be created with just a piece of wire. It is a very interesting experience to give each child about a yard length of soft stove pipe wire and permit him to carry out his ideas in this material. The thinness of the wire and its flexibility will send the child off in entirely new directions seeking and exploring with this new material. This is a desirable activity especially in the upper elementary grades where children are becoming conscious of joints and bends such as knees and elbows in their drawing and painting. We now find a material which allows them to bend at the knees and the ankles and the wrists and at the elbows, a material which lends itself to a greater flexibility than any other material which they have used before. This is a sort of sculpturing which permits the figure to throw the ball and quickly be bent in time to be the catcher. Wire sculpture lends itself to a sort of action sketching in three dimensions with a greater consciousness and awareness of movement and unconsciously a greater sensitivity. About the easiest wire to use for boys and girls is aluminum wire. This is very economical, extremely pliable, and never corrodes. The teacher can generally get a good supply of wire for sculpture and other activities simply by asking the boys in her class who are

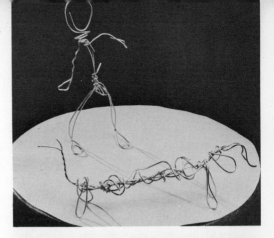

For children wire is meant to be bent or twisted. Wire provides a completely different kind of three-dimensional experience which is challenging and exciting. Because the forms can always be changed, there is allowance for much freedom in thinking and creating.

Each material presents a completely new set of problems and ultimately new solutions. The soda straw or toothpick sculpture invites a unique approach since it cannot be treated like wire, clay, or any other material. Within its limits it brings forth highly individualized treatments.

newsboys to save the wire which binds their bundles of newspapers together. As a rule, such a request for wire to a group of elementary school boys brings a response which is overwhelming.

Wire sculptures are made more attractive if they can be mounted upon a small piece of wood which the children can sand and wax, stain or paint.

Try Tooth Picks or Soda Straws

Tooth pick sculpture is another type of line sculpture which is extremely fascinating to boys and girls in the upper elementary grades and in the junior and senior high school. There is probably no activity in which the child engages in his creative work which seems to hold a greater fascination. The children become completely engrossed in building with tooth picks and model airplane cement. This is one material which seems to be a stimulus in itself. It is interesting to watch children who are given these materials and to observe the different methods with which they work. Some will simply begin with a triangle, develop it into a prism and allow it to grow in all directions into a construction of planes and lines and sometimes closed forms.

It seems unimportant to the child as he builds to state what he is building or to be concerned with any conscious reason for building other than that it seems to satisfy an urge to create something new and something different. Some children who work with tooth picks seem concerned only when making something that is realistic and which can be recognized. This is perfectly permissible and even desirable since the limitations placed upon the child by the materials will help him to develop new and different concepts. The teacher may stimulate the children even further by providing small bits of cellophane or colored papers which the children can sometimes use to define a plane. The same sort of construction can be done with soda straws or colored tooth picks. In working with the airplane cement it is a good idea to work on pieces of waxed paper since cemented objects will not adhere to the waxed surface.

Now White Soap

Probably the most widely publicized of all the sculpturing materials in the elementary school is soap. This by no means implies that it is the best sculpturing material, but good quality white soap lends itself to beautiful carving with a minimum of equipment. An ordinary paring knife, a paper clip, a bobby pin or some tooth picks provide all the tools necessary to do a good job in soap carving. Soap carving should only be done in the upper elementary grades and junior and senior high school because the nature of the material is such that it can be used only successfully where it is consciously approached, that is the child must plan and conceive his figure quite carefully before doing any cutting for a miscut in soap carving can be disastrous so far as the carving is concerned. In the same way that the teacher had to place limitations upon the children in working in ordinary clay, confining them to bulky, heavy, figures, she must now guide the children in planning and designing their sculptures so that they can be handled with a minimum of accidents. Small spindly parts, like very thin legs or a thin tail on an animal, should be discouraged. Sometimes a broken part can be refastened with a small amount of moisture softening both edges of the soap where it is to be joined. This is not always successful. To imply that soap is not a good sculpturing material would be wrong. For some children it provides the most satisfying sort of medium in which to work, especially those children who are interested in working small and carefully. For others, it can be a source of frustration. When this is the case, however, it is the responsibility of the teacher to discover what other types of sculpture better serve that type of child, perhaps wire or tooth picks or one of the other materials which will be later described.

Paraffin or Wax

Paraffin is an extremely fine sculpturing material which lends itself to the ordinary classroom use and yet can be finished in a beautiful manner. Generally, paraffin is purchased in one-pound packages which consists of four one-quarter pound blocks or slabs. The slabs can be used as they are for very interesting relief carving at almost any grade level, but some of the most interesting results come from fusing the four blocks into a solid mass, sometimes with the addition of a small amount of color provided by a wax crayon melted along with the paraffin. It is not difficult to fuse the four blocks if a hot plate is available. The bottom of the waxed carton is carefully sealed with masking tape or gummed tape and placed in a container of cold water. One block is removed and melted and the remaining three separated slightly. The melted block is poured into the box, fusing the three remaining blocks. If the carton should leak slightly the cold water immediately will harden the paraffin, thereby stopping the leak. At a later time the carton is removed and the paraffin can be carved. As is the case, generally, in sculpturing, the shape of the block determines what is to be carved. It is a very good plan to have the children begin the paraffin block with no conscious plan thus allowing the feel of the material to determine the outcome. Very often the paraffin lends itself to the creation of abstract sculptures in which the children create beautiful forms which are nice to look at as well as to feel. Paraffin is fairly sturdy. It permits quite intricate cutting if the child desires to go into detail or if the child is working in a realistic direction but, like soap, it is difficult to repair but not impossible. When all the cutting is complete the paraffin can be smoothed by rubbing it with a rounded stick such as a tongue depressor or a lollypop stick or an orange stick. It can be brought to an almost translucent polish by rubbing it with a stick or smooth piece of cloth, or even the fingers.

Sometimes the addition of a small amount of color by dropping a piece of wax crayon into the melted paraffin, will cause the color to run through the block in a very irregular fashion. This in itself can suggest what shall be cut away and what shall remain. Sometimes the child sees in the color that flows through the block the image of what he wishes to create. Old wax candles or

A variety of sizes and shapes are possible by the use of waxed containers such as milk cartons and hot drink containers. This project is best used with small groups or individuals since the melting process is slow and needs constant attention. Wax can easily catch on fire if spilled on to the hot plate. An improvised double boiler is the safest method.

unbleached beeswax can be melted and added to the paraffin for interesting color. Occasionally, if the whole pound of paraffin is melted and poured back into the box, very minute air bubbles will remain throughout the paraffin bringing a rich appearance to the surface.

Concrete and Zonolite

In recent years an art teacher developed one of the most interesting of all sculpturing materials. This is an entirely permanent material and yet extremely easy to make and easy to use in most classrooms. This sculpturing material is made from a combination of cement and Zonolite. Zonolite is a concrete aggregate made of mica, a very lightweight mineral substance. It is frequently advertised as an insulating material as well. Both the cement and Zonolite can be purchased from any lumber yard or home supply store. For elementary level children a good beginning mixture consists of four parts of Zonolite and one part of dry cement. These are mixed together dry and then enough water added to get it into a moist or fluid state. An ordinary mop bucket or lard can will serve very well as a mixing container. When the mixture is in a fluid state it can be poured into a large cardboard carton. It is a good idea to place the cardboard carton inside a larger cardboard carton on the first attempt in case the teacher adds too much water and the excess moisture weakens the side walls of the inner

The use of a Zonolite-cement mixture provides an opportunity for a true sculpturing experience with a minimum of special preparation and equipment. Other plaster and cement aggregates can be used with the cement.

box thus causing them to break down. If old newspapers have been wadded up between the walls of the two cartons, this will provide ample strength to keep the inner walls from collapsing. This mixture is allowed to harden or to set for about 24 hours. The box is then removed and the Zonolite-cement block can then be sawed into blocks of whatever size the teacher wishes. A good beginning size might be 5″ × 5″ × 8″ or 6″ × 6″ × 10″. This mixture can be cut with the simplest sort of tools—an ordinary kitchen or paring knife, an old hack saw blade, a wood rasp and an old screw driver will provide all the tools needed to do a good job. This mixture is very light and is, of course, extremely easy to cut. (When the child has created sculptured forms or a sculptured figure and it has been allowed to dry for several weeks, it will turn light grey and have a rock-like appearance, and is quite permanent.) For the older students, junior and senior high school, the same materials may be used and a finer texture created by cutting down on the quantity of Zonolite in the mixture. As the proportion of Zonolite is decreased, the density of the cast block increases in proportion as does its hardness. This, of course, implies that different tools will be required with the harder blocks. An ordinary cold chisel, which could be purchased from any dime store, and an ordinary hammer will serve for this type of carving.

As a rule, the classroom does not provide adequate facilities for each child to be carving at the same time. It is a good plan to set up a carving table or a carving corner and allow one or two children to work at a time. Have each child bring in a cardboard carton and when he is ready to start carving fix the side walls of the carton. Now he can work with his sculpture always inside the box so that dirt and chips which are cut away remain in the box. When the piece is entirely finished the box can be carried out of the building or to the trash heap and disposed of without any of the dirt ever reaching the classroom floor. This procedure is almost essential if the classroom teacher desires to have the boys and girls work in carving plaster.

The procedure for plaster is essentially the same as that for Zonolite except that the plaster creates much more dirt and dust in the room and is extremely difficult to clean from the containers once it has set, while the container, such as a bucket, that has been used to mix Zonolite can be easily rinsed out and left in perfect condition. A container which has been used to mix plaster in is extremely difficult to clean as the plaster sets up hard very rapidly. Plaster carving can be used most effectively in the junior and senior high school but then only under very controlled situations.

Relief in Plaster

Plaster plaques or plaster reliefs are very easily created in the upper elementary grades and junior high school. Each child can bring a gift box to school in which to make his plaque. Plasticene is patted or rolled flat and the entire bottom of the child's box is covered with about a one-half inch thick layer of plasticene. The children can work their ideas out directly on this flat plasticene surface. If his first idea doesn't work out satisfactorily, the whole surface can be smoothed out again for a new start. The teacher may wish to have them work

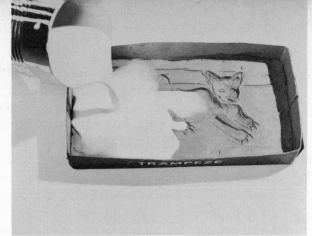

out their ideas first with chalks or crayons on paper. The steps which follow are not easily explained to children unless the teacher has prepared a sample for illustrative purposes and perhaps has a finished plaque from another class or even one which she has made herself. The children can then begin to dig directly in the plasticene using tools improvised from tongue depressor sticks which have been split lengthwise. Into the plasticene they carve, going deep in some spots, remaining shallow in others, until they have expressed their ideas as fully and originally as possible in this material. The plasticene can then be given a very thin coat of vaseline; however, this is not absolutely necessary as oil is already in the plasticene mixture. It does, however, prevent bits of plaster from adhering to the plasticene and causing it to be dirty. The next step involves the mixing of plaster of paris in a container, such as a plastic wash basin or plastic mixing bowl, or an old #10 tin can and pouring the plaster on to the plasticene carvings to a thickness of one-half to three-quarter inches. While the plaster is still wet the child can insert a loop of soft wire near the top of the back for hanging purposes. If the teacher will encourage the children to jostle or jiggle the boxes slightly while the plaster is still liquid, this will cause any air bubbles which might have been trapped in the plaster to rise to the top, insuring a more uniform quality of plaster plaque. When the plaques have dried over night the boxes can be torn away and the plaster plaque lifted away from the plasticene mold. Slight imperfections might be noted at this time and they can be carefully carved away with an ordinary paring knife or, in some instances, a small bit of sand paper can be used to smooth down areas which seem to need a smoothing treatment. After the plaques have dried for several days they can be given a very light sanding to remove all traces of the vaseline which might have some negative affect on future painting operations. And now the plaques are ready for painting. Ordinary water paints, tempera paints, enamels or oil based paints are all satisfactory for finishing this project. The teacher will find the children very excited about this project and wanting to do it over again.

Relief in Soft Wood

If the classroom has working space which provides opportunity for working with tools, interesting relief sculptures can be made by boys and girls in the middle and upper elementary grades. These are worked out most successfully on pieces of soft wood such as white pine which is about three-quarters to one inch thick. The child plans a simple design or figure in the center of his board including as few details as possible. This can be sketched on the surface of the board with a soft pencil. He may indicate with shading or a process of filling in with his pencil those areas which are to be cut away. It is a good practice then to nail or to fasten securely with "C" clamps the piece of wood to the surface of the work bench. This permits the child to concentrate entirely upon his project and does away with the frustrations which accompany shifting and sliding boards. The youngster can then begin to work using one-quarter inch and one-half inch wood gouges and a wooden mallet. With very little practice the child

Pieces of soft wood should be fastened firmly in place so that the child can concentrate on the cutting and not be constantly distracted by the shifting of the piece.

quickly learns to use these tools effectively. There is something very exciting and thrilling, especially to boys, in the process of carving wood, cutting away bit by bit and feeling the wood give under the blows. If there is one especially sharp gouge for the classroom it can be kept for hand finishing—that is, using the gouge in both hands without using the mallet. If it seems necessary to sand the carving at the end of the cutting, the child should be allowed to do so. Finally, the piece can be finished by using ordinary paste wax mixed with a small amount of oil paint, if staining is desired. There are oil waxes containing pigments which will provide fine, rich finishes. Several coats of wax and lots of polishing with a soft cloth brings out a very rich lustre in children's carvings.

In the Round

Large solid chunks of balsa wood lend themselves to wood carvings for upper elementary and junior and senior high school children. Since balsa wood is so very soft it can be easily cut but requires especially sharp cutting edges in order to prevent crushing the wood. Successful small carvings can be done with balsa wood with nothing more than single edge razor blades. However, to successfully proceed with razor blades on balsa wood, the teacher must take time to show the boys and girls methods of slicing out the portions of wood which they wish to remove. With a small amount of practice most children can learn to smoothly remove pieces of the balsa wood and are able to produce fine carvings. As in the case of simple relief carvings, children can either sand their finished product and give it a good finish with a coat of paste wax or can allow the cutting marks to remain.

A project in carving can be the direct outgrowth of the study of another culture. (Courtesy Arts and Activities and Ruth Whorl, Akron, Ohio.)

Newspaper and Zonolite

Newspaper and Zonolite can combine to give one of the richest results in modeling. An excellent modeling material can be made by shredding newspaper and soaking it until it is very pulpy, then adding to this pulp a sizable quantity of wallpaper paste and quantities of dry Zonolite. This mixture can be used for building over an armature in the same way modeling clay would be used when working on an armature but when it dries it has a very unusual, rich textural quality quite unlike any other papier mache. It has a richness in color which requires no painting and becomes permanently hard and very strong. Because of the ease of obtaining the materials for this particular modeling experience, rather large pieces can be made at a very small cost. Simple armatures can be made of sticks and wires fastened to wooden bases or of tightly rolled coils of newspaper into which lengths of coat hanger wire have been inserted. Large, bulky masses can be created by wadding up large pieces of newspaper and simply tying them into place with ordinary string, then building on the surface of this with the papier mache-Zonolite mixture. It is always good when engaging in a project of this sort to make sure that the armature or framework is strong enough structurally to carry through the whole process without any breakdowns. As a rule, a flat piece of board, which can serve as a base, should be used to fasten the armature so that toppling or falling will be prevented. The few minutes spent developing a good foundation or structure will be more than overcome in time saved on later steps and disappointments and frustrations which are by-passed as a result of careful planning.

And Whittle

Whittling is a form of sculpture which is sometimes overlooked in our arts-crafts programs. Many satisfying hours can be passed whittling interesting figures and objects with a sharp pocket knife and a piece of soft, close-grained wood. The scrap box in the local lumber yard will provide enough interesting

Soft wood pieces, twigs, or branches are good for whittling. A small coping saw can hasten some of the larger cuts that may be tedious with a pocket knife. A well-carved walking stick made from a branch can become a child's work of art.

pieces of soft wood for a whole class of youngsters to do their sculpturing with pocket knives. A simple project like whittling can provide many opportunities for creative problem solving in which the child must adapt his ideas or his desire to express ideas to the limitations of the wood and of the pocket knife. The teacher should exercise care not to fall prey to the numerous stereotypes which exist in whittling. There are really only two basic rules to think of: keep the ideas simple and original, and keep the knives sharp.

Repousse

Repousse is relief modeling in metal foils. In this project, as in most crafts, the work develops out of a good motivation which deals with expressing something rather than the learning of a new process. This work in metal foils involves a whole new set of problems and solutions. First, the manipulation of the metal is unlike any other craft experience; secondly, the whole project is worked from the back side of the metal, or perhaps it would be more accurate to say that the major part of the problem is solved from the reverse side. Metal foils such as copper, aluminum and brass can be purchased from most school supply or art supply stores. It may be sold either by size or by weight, aluminum being the lightest, the least expensive, and easiest to work. However, the copper and brass are the more attractive when finished.

This project might begin with chalk drawings of whatever experience has been chosen to be illustrated. Perhaps it is one of "playing with your pet" or "playing games at recess." The chalk drawings will cause the child to work larger and with less detail thus providing a drawing which will better be adapted to the foil. When the drawings are ready and have been discussed by teacher and child for aptness, the piece of foil is placed directly beneath the drawing, which is traced over with a pencil point in order to leave an impression on the foil. Now the foil is turned over and parts of the drawing are pressed out slowly and carefully by placing the foil on a soft stack of newspapers and rubbing over the part with a blunt stick. A tongue depressor which has been split lengthwise makes an excellent tool for this purpose. Some areas may be pushed out quite far while others remain fairly low. The depth of the depression depends upon the amount of pressure applied to the stick and the number of times it is gone over. When the entire design has been pushed out the foil may be turned over and some work done on the top side. Some areas may be improved by creating textured surfaces

A small stick and a soft pad of paper is all the equipment necessary for metal repousse work.

Copper foil provides an opportunity to express an experience in a new way. This piece by an eleven year old child shows a group of children "cracking the whip" on the skating pond.

where they have not been pushed out or raised. This could be accomplished by finding something to tamp with, such as a nail head, pencil point, bobby pin, or some other small item.

To insure that no damage can occur to the raised surface or the finished piece, the back can be filled with soft modeling clay. This will prevent any raised surface from being pushed in if accidentally pushed or bumped. Now the finished foil can be fastened to a piece of plywood or wall board. Special nails called escutcheon pins can be purchased in aluminum, brass or copper for fastening to the boards; often the foils are just stapled to the wall board, or carpet tacks or gimp nails used on the wood. The foil can be brightly polished with steel wool and the wood stained and waxed or the wallboard painted with any type of paint.

Repousse is exceptionally well liked by the children of the upper elementary grades and the junior high school but it is a process which is often representative of the worst in art and industrial arts education for it is in this process that one sees the most stereotyped work such as palm trees, sailing boats, jumping fish, bird dogs and the like. This is generally the result of the procedure becoming the thing and the motivation being overlooked. This should never be the case in good education. What is said with any medium is of greater importance than how it is said.

And in Conclusion

The opportunities for modeling and sculpturing are limitless. While there appear to be many common or universal materials for modeling and sculpturing, there are many fine local materials available to teachers in different parts of the country. In some areas lava-type stones can be found which are very satisfactory for carving. In other areas where scrap materials are readily available teachers may find sizable scraps of foam glass used in large construction projects. Older children can make excellent sculptures from fire brick where material of this sort is available. It is important that teachers be alert to find the materials which exist in their own localities and use whatever they might find. The most imaginative and the most creative programs begin at home and not in the art supply catalogues.

TRY MAKING PRINTS

3

PROCESSES which allow the child to reproduce the designs which he creates are important to include in the arts and crafts program even for the very young child. Small children can often be found creating designs all over a sidewalk or wall merely by dipping their hands into mud or dirt and making a series of orderly or sometimes chaotic prints. Other times children are seen at the beaches creating designs with sticks, their sand pails, shovel handles or even with their feet in the soft moist sand. This desire to design by reproducing one shape over and over seems natural with children and therefore should be utilized. This unconscious designing can be seen in the drawing or painting processes where many times boys and girls repeat the same design over and over thereby creating an excellent pattern. The child may draw a tree over and over in a picture and then say, "See, I have made a forest." However, this desire should not be confused with the fact that some children who are emotionally or creatively blocked are able to conceive only one idea and therefore make it over and over again without any variations, thus producing stereotypes.

With Sticks and Stuff

Perhaps the most widely used of these processes in the lower grades of the elementary school is that of stick printing. For this process small blocks of wood, sometimes capped with felt, of various sizes and shapes, are dipped or pressed against an ink pad and then pressed onto a piece of paper. Sets of this sort can be purchased commercially but it is much more interesting for the children to make sets of their own. A search of a wood scrap box plus a variety of bottle caps, jar lids, wooden spools, clothes pins, and other interestingly shaped objects will provide a more challenging set of instruments than the standard circles, squares, and triangles usually provided in the kits. The teacher may wish to combine new shapes with parts of a commercial kit.

And Potatoes and Carrots

Perhaps even more challenging is the development of a design by the child himself, using a vegetable as the printing tool. Children can bring in a carrot, turnip, or potato from home. This is then sliced in half, creating two smooth surfaces on which to design. Each surface may be cut with simple, dull tools. An old paring knife will serve very well. The child simply cuts away some parts of the smooth surface leaving the remainder as the surface which will print. Regardless of the child's ability to create "good" designs in the sense that the

A potato, turnip, or carrot are all effective for simple printing. A small paring knife and some tempera paints are the only other necessary materials.

teacher normally desires, any design which he creates will be both interesting and attractive if printed in a rhythmic and systematic way. The teacher may stress the value of bringing order into the printing process but without worrying too much about the design which the child creates on his vegetable. A good way to proceed with very small children is to have the potato "walk" with nice even steps across the paper and when it gets to the other side it may walk back again. This "walking" across the paper will create an even sort of rhythm which will be orderly and interesting after three or four lines have been developed.

Print with Modeling Clay

One of the best and one of the easiest printing surfaces for small children is ordinary plastic modeling clay of the type commonly known as plasticine. This clay can be pounded into small flat cakes about an inch thick and carved directly on the flat surface with a bobby pin or small pointed stick which removes portions of the clay. The ease in preparing a block for printing leads to very direct prints which resemble the drawings of the children perhaps more closely than other types of prints. When the design or picture is prepared on the surface it can be smoothed slightly to remove any crumbs of clay that may remain on the surface. Then it can be inked with a rubber brayer just like a linoleum block and printed by pressing it onto paper which is resting on a pad of newspaper. It is easier to get good clear prints when a padded surface, such as twenty or thirty thicknesses of newspaper, is under the paper on which the print is made.

Plastic modeling clay is pressed upon a paper pad which has been soaked in water and covered with tempera. The "inked" clay is then pressed on porous paper for clear, bright prints.

Another method of printing which is probably preferable to the brayer method is the use of the paint pad which is described later in this chapter. This allows for much more rapid printing and a good deal less equipment. When the printing experience is complete the paints can be washed from the surface of the modeling clay and it can be returned to its storage place for the next use which might be found for it. Some of the paint will remain, but it will not affect the future usefulness of the clay.

Or an Old Inner Tube

If an even more controlled design is desired, one which is similar to a block print, the teacher or a child might obtain on old inner tube from a nearby gas station or garage. There is generally a pile of discarded ones in the rubbish heap behind any gas station. This can be cut into pieces about five inches square, smaller or larger depending upon the project. Each child is given a square with which to work. The children may sketch their ideas directly onto the inner tube with chalk and then cut out the designs with ordinary classroom scissors. The rubber design is then glued to blocks of scrap wood of any thickness. A child can print with this much in the same way he would with a rubber stamp or potato. If a cleaner more accurate print is desired, especially in the upper elementary grades or the junior high school, the block print may be inked with blockprinting ink rolled on with a rubber brayer. A print can be made by placing the inked block on a piece of clean paper and standing on it, or it can be tapped with a mallet or hammer. Either a water base or an oil base blockprinting ink is satisfactory. The teacher may wish to combine this inner tube method with some of the other methods which will be described later in this chapter.

You'll Need a Pad

A good printing pad for the vegetable and stick prints can be made by using about twenty thicknesses of newspaper cut about 9 × 12 inches, saturated with water, and sprinkled with dry powder paints or moist tempera paints. Using this the child can press the potato against the pad, picking up color, then press the

The use of waste or scrap materials is challenging. Shown here are prints made from pieces of an old inner tube and ones made from cotton cord which has been glued to pieces of wood. Pieces of cardboard which are glued to wood can make excellent prints.

potato firmly against the paper on which he is printing. This process is repeated with each print.

Using these processes of reproduction with small children, the children might decorate wrapping papers at Christmas time; they might make waste baskets by covering old ice cream cartons; or perhaps they might make notebook or story book covers.

Make a Paper Stencil

Still another way of making prints using a minimum of materials is working with paper stencils. Each child can be given four or five pieces of drawing paper about four inches square. The children can cut some holes of various sizes and shapes into the centers of each piece, using their scissors. It is good to limit each piece to one hole or shape. When these are cut, each child may be given a piece of Kleenex, a small piece of cotton, or a small patch of wool cloth. The Kleenex, cotton, or cloth is rubbed on a piece of colored chalk, picking up enough dust to stencil. One of the shapes is selected and placed upon the paper on which the stencil design is to go. The child carefully rubs his Kleenex making strokes from the stencil paper toward the center of the opening which has been cut. He goes all around the edge of the opening until the paper beneath it has a good clear print. The teacher might encourage the children to repeat this same shape clear across the paper even making two or three rows before returning to the first print which he made. Now the child may combine a new shape with the first shape but using a new color, again repeating the second color as he did in the first stencil. To make two or three rows such as this brings out the value of rhythm and repetition to the child without the teacher's having to stress the words or to enforce rules or principles. After this has been accomplished the teacher may wish to have the children try all their shapes or to create some new ones until they are able to decide on the combination which they like best. Some of the children may even try to combine some of their shapes to create realistic symbols; others will remain very happy to create abstractions. This chalk and stencil method can be used at any age level. The older children will make more complex stencils and use a greater number of colors. Junior and senior high school children can render quite complex and interesting Christmas cards or program covers using this same procedure. Here however, the children will probably cut their stencils with an X-acto knife or razor blade to insure more accurate and sharper edges.

Change to Crayons

This same stencil procedure can be used with wax crayons in place of chalks. The crayons are rubbed directly onto the stencil. These stencils can be used very effectively on pieces of unbleached muslin or any other cotton material with a smooth surface. The children can make very attractive door and wall hangings for the classroom, or they may even make drapes or window curtains for the classroom. The most interesting classrooms are the ones in which the children have a part in the planning and decorating. Nothing is so cold as the appearance of a classroom with no evidence of the children who occupy it. If the crayon is a good quality wax crayon it can be pressed rather permanently into the cloth by using a warm iron and will survive a good number of careful washings with lukewarm water.

Or Paints

The teacher of the middle and upper elementary grades or the junior high school may wish to use the stencil method but in a somewhat different manner. Moist paints can be used to do the stenciling. Moist paints give a sharp and brilliant appearance to the stencil and lend themselves to greater detail. With moist paints the stencil process is essentially the same with the exception that the paper from which the stencil is cut must be a waterproof type. There are good waxed stencil papers available commercially which are not only water-

Stenciling can be done with chalks, crayons, tempera, and textile paints using very simple procedures with small children and problems of increasing difficulty with older ones.

proof but are translucent enough to permit good registry* where more than one color is being used. However, for the teacher who operates her program on a limited budget, there is an adequate substitute. Almost every school system has a mimeograph machine in its main office, or some business establishment in town may have one. On the back of every mimeograph stencil there is a heavy waxed paper which is torn off when the stencil is placed on the mimeograph machine. These waxed backs which are normally thrown away make an excellent stencil paper both for water soluble and oil based paints.

In using moist paints it is necessary to have stiff bristle brushes with which to stencil. Stencil brushes which are sold commercially are the best, but the teacher can make a substitute from a small enamel brush by cutting the bristles off

---

* Getting each color correctly in its place.

carefully with a razor blade about ¾ inch below the ferrule or metal band which holds the bristle. By experimenting with the stencil brush and paint, the child can determine the correct amount of paint necessary and the best technique to stroke his design. The children should be encouraged to work with a very dry brush which seems to be almost out of color, and to build up the color with numerous strokes rather than using one very moist stroke. If the brush is too moist, the color will seep under the edges of the stencil and spread unpleasantly, ruining the smooth clean edge desired. Any type of water paints can be used for this sort of stenciling. Upper elementary grade and junior high school children will enjoy making Christmas cards, programs, placemats for parties, and other projects which require a reproductive process.

Make It for Keeps

Having mastered the stencil method, the children may wish to put their newly discovered skills to work on a more permanent project. Excellent textile paints are available now which are within the budget limitations of most schools. These paints are so simple to use that no previous experience or special technical knowledge is necessary to use them and they are of such quality that they could be used successfully even in a commercial enterprise. The teacher who instructs her children carefully and who encourages sound practices of economy, care of materials and equipment, will find that a very small amount of paint will go far in textile painting. It is natural for children in the upper elementary and junior high school to be interested in clothing and decoration; therefore the classroom can serve excellently as a laboratory for experiments in problems designed to satisfy this natural interest. Using textile paint, children can print very beautiful window drapes, wall hangings, placemats, napkins, scarves, and other small items.

And Make It Their Own

Teachers should be alert to see that children of any age level develop their own designs when stenciling and block printing. There is always a danger of the children copying stereotyped designs or even using ready cut patterns which come in some sets of paints. The use of either of these places definite limitations on the child's chances of developing creatively. To depend upon the design of another is only fostering a feeling of dependence which will continue to grow until the child has a complete feeling of inadequacy and finds himself unable to think or create for himself. He will always need to depend upon the ideas and thoughts of others. At no time should the product become more important than the child. It is more important to think of what the craft can do for the child rather than what the child can do to the craft.

Have You Spattered?

Spatter painting or printing is a process which permits a wide variety of experiments in design. The process is so fast and fascinating that seldom can a child be found who is not completely carried away by the project. Only very simple equipment is needed to begin spatter painting.

Have the children find an old toothbrush. Several for one room will probably be enough, as only one or two children work at a time on this process. Other than the toothbrush, the teacher needs only a small amount of water paint and some paper on which to make the painting. The process is one of spraying paint with the toothbrush. A knife blade or other straight edged object is pulled across the top of the brush allowing the bristles to snap forward throwing small particles of paint onto the paper. The design is created by placing small flat objects or shapes upon the paper which prevent the spray from striking the paper, leaving the shapes free of paint spray and the rest of the paper covered with small spatters or flecks of paint. This, of course, has endless possibilities in that one color may be superimposed on another and any variety of shapes can be used. Perhaps its widest use is spatter painting nature forms. In this, the child gathers interesting shapes of leaves, twigs, weeds, grasses, and other things from nature. Any grown-over vacant lot or field is an ideal hunting ground for the beautiful forms of nature. Finding beauty in nature such as this is a project which is valuable in itself. The child takes some of his objects and arranges them on his paper. When he feels that he has an interesting arrangement on his paper,

The spatter print resembles air-brush drawing and is based on the same principle, that of spraying minute particles of paint on to a surface which is partially covered by a stencil.

he places the paper and arrangement on the floor which has been covered with a number of sheets of newspaper. He dips his old toothbrush into some paint, shakes off the excess and begins to spatter his design by gently pulling a knife blade across the bristles of the brush which has been aimed at the design. After a few trials the children will learn just how much paint and of what consistency to use, as well as the amount of pressure to put on their knife strokes. By experimenting he will gain rather good control of the spray. This control permits intensifying the spray in some areas and keeping it light in others. After spraying his design, he permits it to dry, then lifts away the nature shapes. He may find that one form has overlapped another, thus destroying the shapes of both; he may find some areas which seem unnecessarily bare. The child may begin to have some feeling for good composition on his paper without the teacher ever having to mention the word "composition."

The nature forms should be only a beginning for the class, who should be encouraged to find all sorts of interesting shapes and forms in their environment, perhaps to develop some completely abstract spatter paintings. Then again, some children may wish to use this form of painting to develop a realistic concept. If this is the case, the children should be permitted to make such attempts. Again the limitations of the medium will cause them to deviate from their usual drawing and painting techniques.

After the class has begun such a project, some of the more inventive children will conceive of better ways of spattering such as building a spatter box by covering the bottom of an old chalk box or cigar box with a piece of window screening. This spatter box is used by rubbing a small brush like a fingernail brush or very small scrubbing brush across the screening, thus spraying the area beneath it. Often the teacher will find a child in the classroom who may seem limited in his creative ability according to standards expected in drawing or painting, but who can think up a most ingenious spatter box. His creative efforts are being channeled into a new direction. The creative abilities of children are not always shown in the same ways, nor do they develop at the same rate.

Anything Is Possible

The children of the upper elementary grades or of the junior or senior high school can make some excellent prints if there is any sort of press available in their school system. The children use a fairly heavy piece of cardboard, a piece of old poster board, or a piece of newsboard which they cover with a very heavy coat of shellac. While the shellac is moist or tacky, a design is developed by placing pieces of string, seeds, rice, straw, bits of burlap, weeds, or any other available materials on the shellac-covered cardboard. When these have become well set in the shellac an inked brayer or roller may be rolled across the surface touching all the raised parts and perhaps some of the flat areas. This inked design is covered with a piece of drawing paper, placed in the press, and pressure

applied. When the paper is withdrawn it will have a printed impression of the design. A few experiments of this sort will begin to open up endless possibilities to the class and will serve as a point of departure for many diversified problems.

This process can serve as a background in combination with some of the other printing processes described in this chapter. Background prints might be conceived as such and developed especially for that purpose. For example, an interesting background might be developed by casually dropping a piece of wet cheesecloth onto the shellacked surface and permitting it to dry just as it falls. This when inked will provide an excellent textural background when printed in the manner previously described. Often the cheesecloth or a piece of burlap will serve as a print itself if the arrangement is interesting. Again in this method some children will attempt a realistic concept; but, as in previous processes, the limitations of the process will provide a new variation quite unlike a drawing concept. Some children may make attempts at profile concepts using string, but the limitations of the string will provide most interesting results.

Like a Shirt Caught on the Wringer

Another variation of printing may be made by using a brayer or roller which is tacky or sticky with printing ink. By dropping several pieces of string at random and slowly running the brayer over them, the string will adhere to the brayer because of the stickiness. The brayer with string attached can be run across the ink plate and then across a paper. Each time the roller revolves it will leave an impression of the string adhered to it, thus creating an interesting, dynamic design over and over. This type of printing may serve as a print in

Cotton cord or heavy twine caught around the roller of a brayer makes an interesting print variation.

itself, as the basis for a future planned design, or as a background for block printing. By experimenting the teacher and children will find that there are many variations of this type of printing. Perhaps scraps of paper could be dropped instead of the pieces of string, or a combination of paper and strings used.

Stick to It

A very interesting print can be made using an ordinary piece of window glass or a block of linoleum tile on which Duco cement or a cement of a similar sort has been dripped rather freely, directly from the tube. Using the clear glass, the children may sometimes want to make a rather free sketch which they place beneath the glass and try to follow with the drips from the cement tube. Some may prefer to work entirely spontaneously, developing the design as they freely drip the cement. After the cement sets for a day, the glass plate or tile, as the case may be, is inked in the same manner that a block print is inked. The ink has a tendency to adhere to the raised surface of the cement and to pass over the plain glass. A piece of paper is placed over the plate and rubbed with the back of a spoon or the rounded handle of a brush. When the paper is removed the paper will bear an impression of the design created by the cement. Naturally, when making prints from a piece of glass great care must be exercised to keep the glass on a smooth surface and not to place undue pressure on any one spot which might cause it to break. The child can get very interesting variations from the glass plate by merely brushing the color on with a stiff brush, then placing his paper against the plate, rubbing the back of the paper with a hard, smooth object, and pulling away his print. The piece of glass used in cement printing may be easily cleaned by submerging it for a short period in water which will cause the cement to loosen and slip free of the glass.

Monoprints Are Marvelous

Making monoprints is a very exciting process which affords endless variations. Perhaps the easiest method of making monoprints is to use a smooth non-porous surface such as window glass. Most hardware stores which sell window glass have a barrel of small pieces which they usually throw away. Such a barrel generally contains dozens of pieces which are large enough for monoprinting. Usually these can be had for the asking. The teacher must use caution in handling these pieces as the edges are extremely sharp. Using liquid tempera paints, or water-base block printing ink, the children drip various colors from matchsticks, toothpicks, or brush handles, creating interesting designs or pictures on the glass. While the paints are still wet a piece of paper is placed over them and gently rubbed. When the paper is removed, it bears a brilliant impression which is interesting and exciting. Sometimes two prints can be made one after the other but never with exactly the same effect. The child can then drip additional paints on the already used plate or he may wish to wash his plate before making a new print. In beginning monoprints the teacher may wish to limit the children to a fairly small area, say 3″ × 4″ or 4″ × 5″. This will permit them to cut the drawing paper into smaller pieces, thus economizing. Only those prints by each child which seem to be the best should be matted or mounted. Some children will make attempts at realistic interpretations while monoprinting. These children should be encouraged in such experiments, as they will make numerous color discoveries which may carry over into their later work.

Monoprints are interesting in themselves but can also be used as the basis for a painting. Many children like to use ink or paints over them to make a picture.

In all the processes which have been previously described, the teacher should be watching for opportunities to use papers other than the ordinary drawing papers. The children should try some prints on newspapers, pages out of magazines, pieces of wallpaper, paper bags, wrapping papers, or any other types of paper. It is, in fact, a good project to have the children find as many kinds of paper as they can. The gathering and examination of a large variety of types of papers could be an interesting discussion period or could make an interesting display by the class. Imagine the interesting print a child might get by using an old road map as the background for a monoprint or blockprint. In subsequent lessons the children might use some of the variety of their papers for drawing or painting projects. Sometimes the very surface of a paper may suggest the picture which goes on it. This is often true when using an ordinary sheet of newspaper for water color painting. The making of monoprints lends itself to all sorts of interesting discoveries in color and texture which the children may later use in their other arts and crafts activities.

But Try Everything

Whenever the children have been using a brayer and an inked plate for any of the printing processes, the plate can be used before it is cleaned for some experiments. If the glass has been covered all over with block printing inks, a picture or design can be scratched through the ink surface exposing lines of clear glass. A toothpick or other similar simple tool can be used for the scratching. A sheet of paper can be laid over the glass plate and rubbed lightly then removed. The paper will bear a reverse image of the picture which was scratched through the paint.

It is satisfying for a child to carry a many-stepped process through to completion.

Linoleum Prints

Linoleum block printing can be considered a standard process for almost every art program of the secondary schools but it is also found in many good elementary programs. As a result of its wide acceptance it is possible to get good cutting tools and good quality linoleum at most school supply houses. The tools are generally small U or V shaped gouges or chisels which are pushed along the surface of the linoleum removing portions according to the shape of the gouge. Normally, several sets of tools can suffice for a room and the children can work at different times on their projects; however, many schools buy enough to supply each member of a class. Linoleum is another of the processes which sometimes allow the teaching of methods to override the fact that in every process the children have something personal to express. Too often linoleum cuts are used only at the holidays for very trite and stereotyped cards when they can be used effectively at any time during the school year.

Begin with a very strong motivation like a field trip to a poultry house, or view a good film perhaps on some aspect of nature, such as the life of a bumble bee. From this experience have the children select certain parts that interest them and from these develop their linoleum design. This drawing can then be transferred onto the surface of the linoleum. At this point, the teacher must dis-

The classroom should reflect the fact that it is occupied by children. Their linoleum blocks can make excellent drapes or curtains.

cuss methods of handling the tools safely, the problems of cutting away and leaving portions, developing some balance between the dark and white areas, the variety of cuts that are possible, and some ways of creating textures. Especially must she stress personal investigation and inventions of technique by the children. The size of the project depends upon the amount of available linoleum. If there is a limited amount of linoleum there are several methods for doing a more interesting project than just routine cutting and printing of small prints. One way is to use a large sheet of linoleum on which each child draws a part of one common theme such as "we are working in our gardens." This can be handled similarly to a painted or cut paper mural. When the drawings are in place a group discussion will easily take care of empty or overcrowded spots or of things which are too small or too large. The children have a fine intuitive feeling for good design, and group discussion will always aid in any cooperative project.

Now that the plan is complete and agreed upon the children can each carve their portion. Finally a committee of several children can finish all unassigned areas, and perhaps handle backgrounds. This small group will pull the whole design together or unify it. With this type of print the class can make draperies for the room, or each child can bring a piece of cloth such as unbleached muslin and with oil base inks each can make himself a fine wall-hanging for his bedroom. To print these, an old blanket spread out on the floor would make a good printing surface. The block when inked can be placed face down on the muslin,

Twenty-two students helped design and cut this large block print and each made a print on fabric for a wall hanging.

39

the printer slowly shifting his feet until he has covered every inch of the block. This should make a good even print.

Another method involves again common solution of a problem. This time the children work on individual blocks, each developing his own idea. Later each block is printed on one common paper or fabric in an orderly way to develop a type of print mural. Linoleum cutting and printing should allow the child to find here a means of personal expression based upon a good experience. The teaching of good procedures is essential also, for if the child cannot carry out his idea once he has developed it, nothing will be gained. If, on the other hand, nothing is stressed but the procedures of cutting and printing the child may know how to say it well but have nothing to say. Needless to say, the time spent in thinking through a good motivation for such a project will certainly bear quick returns.

Even the Schoolyard Fence

One other interesting background method that children might use is printing with grainy wood. Each child should find a piece of soft grainy wood such as a piece of yellow pine or plywood. When the wood is examined, the child will find that the grain is tougher than the wood between it. This grain will remain standing firm when the soft part is scratched away. This soft area can be scratched away with a knife, a large nail, or wire brush; the process can be hastened if a torch is applied to the surface of the piece of wood charring the whole surface. The soft areas between the grain become charred first and are then easy to remove. With the grain left standing, the board can be inked and printed and will serve as an excellent textural background for a block print of any sort.

Screen Printing—in a Box

The inventiveness and resourcefulness of art teachers have slowly wrought changes and simplifications to the once highly difficult process of screen printing. Only a few years past the process challenged the best of technicians and it was filled with constant frustrations. Today many teachers use screen printing regularly as classroom work. The development of good water-soluble textile paint has made even textile printing simple enough for every school.

For the teacher who is trying to do screen printing with limited facilities and equipment, the following method may prove effective especially if a large number of screens are to be used simultaneously.

The screen is constructed from a gift box of a size suitable for holding a man's shirt or lady's slip. A cut is made about an inch from the edges to remove the center of the box (Fig. 1). A piece of inexpensive organdy (from a dry goods store) is cut large enough to cover the outside of the box including the vertical edges. The organdy is stapled tightly to the box, making sure to avoid wrinkles and creases (Fig. 2).

The box is then covered inside and out with brown kraft gummed tape leaving exposed the center opening (Fig. 3). The teacher should insist on neatness in this phase. After the box is well covered, it is shellacked heavily for waterproofing. Care should be exercised to avoid drops on the center opening. When dry, the screen is all ready for use.

In planning the first design, simplicity in color, detail and composition is essential. Since color registry is a problem, color areas should not be so carefully defined as to be disturbing if slight errors in placement occur. Printing generally begins with the lightest color and ends with the darkest.

The first stencil is cut from mimeograph stencil backs, wax paper or regular silk screen stencil paper. It is made by cutting away only those parts which are to print (Fig. 4).

The screen paint is prepared by mixing Ivory Snow with liquid tempera or a good quality powder tempera with water and Ivory Snow. This should have a stiff consistency, about like pudding (Fig. 5).

Now to the printing! On the desk place a small stack of paper on which to print. Over this stack, place the cut stencil and finally on that place the screen box. Apply a good portion of the first color (about 3 or 4 heaping tablespoonfuls). With pressure, drag the paint across the screen with a small window squeegee or flat tongue depressor, making sure all areas are covered (Fig. 6). (A few practices will help your technique.)

Lift the box from the stack of paper and you will find your print on the top sheet while your stencil has adhered to the bottom of the box (Fig. 7).

The stencil remains here until the color run is complete. The squeegee process is repeated until a sufficient number of prints have been made.

The stencil is removed by peeling it free from the back of the box (Fig. 8). Wipe the screen as clear as possible with a dry cloth followed by a damp cloth or sponge (Fig. 9). Avoid soaking the box in water as it shortens its usefulness. It is impossible to remove all traces of color but this is no problem.

The screen is now ready for a second stencil and color. From this point the process is repeated as often as necessary to complete the design.

Figure 1

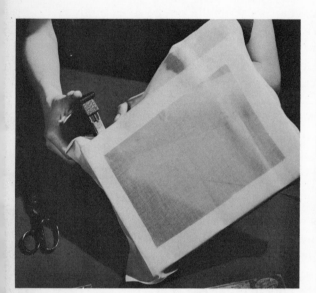

Figure 2   Figure 3

Figure 4   Figure 5

Figure 6   Figure 7

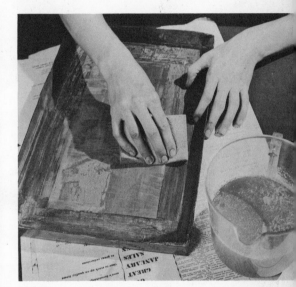

Figure 8   Figure 9

It's Up to You

Whatever the materials the teacher has to work with, the processes of reproduction can be worked into her program. It is up to the teacher to utilize the materials she has on hand and find her own best technique. Limitations in materials should never be the excuse for lack of a good program for often these very limitations are the beginning of the most interesting innovations and result in new and vital arts and crafts programs.

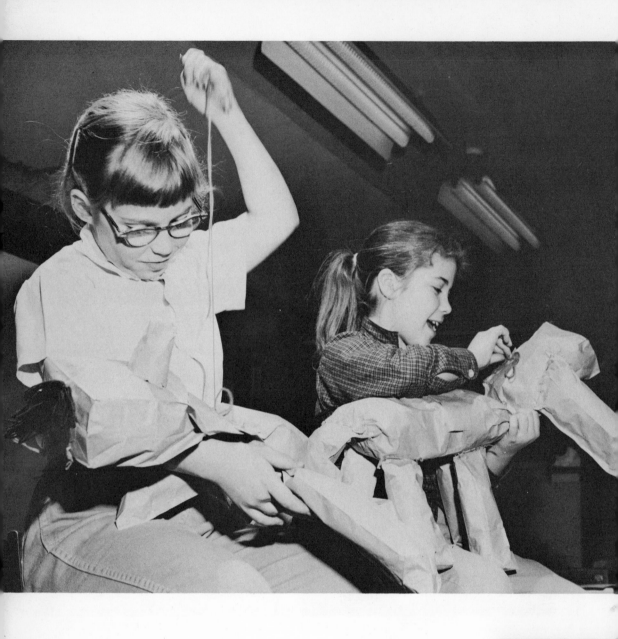

PUPPETS

ARE A MUST

THERE IS probably no greater thrill or sense of satisfaction than that which comes to the teacher who through her planning and efforts finds her pupils unfolding and revealing qualities which had lain dormant. Often these very qualities are not evident because the child lacks confidence in himself or is even unable to communicate his thoughts and feelings for lack of the right medium. In puppetry, the teacher will find many possibilities to enrich most educational situations. Often through the medium of the puppet, the child finds himself able to express thoughts, ideas, and feelings which he otherwise could not. While the puppet may serve as a therapeutic aid, it has many other implications in the field of education. Its wide range of uses and the large variety of types of puppets makes it possible for most teachers in ordinary classroom situations to work with puppetry. Puppetry is a teaching tool which can be used at any age level and can be modified to meet the physical and equipment limitations of even the poorest situations. There is no right way or wrong way to make puppets, but rather there may be a best way for each individual teacher. The teacher has to try the materials which are available and to develop personal puppet techniques. It is good to know a number of ways to make puppets so that they can be used at all age levels without repeating the same types and methods of approach. These should never become repetitious.

To use puppets as a means of correlation is valuable but correlation should never be allowed to become a limitation. Too often attempts at correlation are simply impositions rather than a natural outgrowth of a study unit. There are many valuable personal qualities which puppets help develop.

Start with a Bag

Imagine a first grade class in which the teacher desires to have the children express themselves more freely and imaginatively. From the local grocery store or from the homes, the teacher and children gather enough paper bags to provide one for each child. With scissors, colored papers, and paste, paints, or crayons, the children make a face on the surface of their bag. The teacher should be alert to stimulate the children for an awareness of the facial parts. She may encourage experimentation with the papers for some three dimensional effects and should be ready to accept a wide variety of interpretations. The teacher should be careful to see that the puppet remains a product of the child's own imagination and experience. At this age level more emphasis should be placed on the use of the puppets than on the product which the child is turning out. After each child has completed his puppet, the teacher might suggest the beginning of a story such as the following: "There is a little boy in our neighborhood who is about your age. He has a very bad habit of throwing stones at things.

Even the most simple puppets are worthy of a performance. This young puppeteer awaits her turn.

The other day he threw one over his back fence. Crash! Out comes his neighbor, a very grumpy man! Out comes his mother! The man begins to speak to the boy; the mother speaks to the man. What do you think they are saying? What will the little boy say? Who would like to pretend to be the little boy, the man, the mother? That's fine, now come to the front of the room, put your puppet over your hand and go behind the piano (or screen) and finish the play." At this point the children begin to express themselves. In this way the teacher can develop a play which will go on spontaneously for four or five minutes in which the children will adopt the suggested characters and identify with the problems of the little boy of the play. Teachers will find that frequently boys and girls who, when called to the front of the class to read or talk, can only giggle and laugh or are generally unable to express themselves may become quite at ease in a role in such a play. However, puppetry is no cure-all and should not be expected to do the impossible. At this same age level the teacher might want to develop a greater feeling for group activities. She may separate the children into groups of three, four or five and have each group work out a play of it's own.

Add a Stick

As a variation of the previous puppet the teacher may gather some scrap sticks from the lumber yard or may have one of the older school children gather sticks from the high school woodshop scrap box. These should be about the size of yardsticks but could be thicker or shorter. The rural teacher could cut twigs from a wooded area. On this puppet, the bag should be slipped over the stick and firmly stuffed with wads of newspaper. The open end of the bag is then tied firmly to the stick. If a stapler is available, the bag can be stapled to the stick. Paint the head or make a face with colored papers and paste. If crayons are the only available material for decorating the bag, use them. Perhaps a search of resources will uncover some scrap yarns, wood shavings, buttons, etc. which will enrich the puppet. Encourage the children to search for and discover some new use for old or seemingly useless materials. This exploration in materials and ideas is basic in creative education.

Having completed a head on the stick the children will want to make an appropriate body. If there is no cardboard or oaktag available, the body can be sketched on a piece of newspaper. It can be cut out of about ten thicknesses of newspaper and the edges sealed with paste. The body can then be painted, crayoned or dressed in colored papers. If the teacher is working on a limited budget, she can find an excellent supply of colored paper in the wallpaper books which the local paint, wallpaper and decorator shops discard periodically as styles, prices, and lines change. This body can then be glued or stapled onto the stick. It will have a pleasing effect as the child moves it as he talks. A good practice for the children is to encourage some motion with each word spoken. This type of puppet lends itself to correlated projects especially where children are studying other lands and other peoples. This easy puppet makes it possible to design and duplicate the clothing and costuming of the culture being studied. It lends itself to research at a very early age level. The middle or upper elementary grades are generally the best for this type project since the children of this age have a high interest in clothing and dress.

And a Few More Bags

The common paper bag has endless possibilities in puppet making. In the upper elementary grades it is a good project to make puppets using nothing but paper bags. The children are encouraged to bring in as many types and sizes of bags as they can find and plenty of newspapers for use in stuffing and for clothing. The bags are stuffed with wadded newspapers and stapled or glued shut. If staples are not available the bags can be sewn shut with thread or yarn. Perhaps one child can start with the largest bag that he has for a body. On top of it he may staple or sew a medium size bag which would serve as the head. He then may take a long thin bag and cut it in half lengthwise making two long, very thin bags. Of course he must paste, staple, or glue the open edges together so

Paper bags are quickly transformed into puppets of character with scissors, needle and thread, paint and childhood imagination.

they can be stuffed. These two bags can serve as arms and be attached to the shoulders of the largest bag. The child finds other bags which serve as legs, hands, or feet. If the child is especially skilful he may want to make joints at the knees and elbows. Sometimes little bags will serve as ears or a nose or the child may modify the bags that he has to create other features. This type puppet can simply be suspended by strings from a single stick such as a yardstick which can be jiggled along to give the feeling of walking or moving. Another child in the same group might find a long thin bag which would serve as a body of an animal. He might find bags that he could use or change to serve as legs, tails, ears, or head. He may even make a lower jaw so that his dog can bark or his lion can bite. Having made the main structures the children can costume or decorate the puppets to satisfy their own desires. At this older age level the children are apt to be very inventive and find many materials which they can bring from home to serve as the costumes. Children may come in with bits of felt from an old hat which might serve as ears for a dog or they may find a piece of rope that would serve as a tail for a horse or a piece of old lace tablecloth or old window curtains which might serve as a fancy dress. This sort of puppet serves in a rather unique way in dramatizing plays or stories with it. Instead of having the puppetteers hidden behind a screen or stage, the children simply walk and move with their puppets in full view of the audience. This is significant in that the child no longer is protected by the stage or puppet. He is communicating in full view of his peers. The amazing part of such a performance is the fact that soon after the presentation begins the audience becomes unaware of the children who manipulate the puppets and they become interested only in the puppets. Likewise, the children who operate the puppets soon lose any fear of the audience and identify only with the role of the puppet.

Puppets can help develop confidence and poise in communication.

When time is limited, the tube puppet can be quickly constructed and effectively used.

Or Try a Tube

Another interesting and effective type of puppet is the cylinder or tube puppet. Children may begin with a piece of 9″ × 12″ or 12″ × 18″ drawing or construction paper and roll it into a cylinder. Where the ends meet it is stapled or glued so that it holds its form. This tube then serves as the head of the puppet. Some children will make long thin tubes while others will make short squat ones. Some may even deviate from the cylinder and choose to make a cone shape or a modification of the cone shape. Such deviations should be encouraged.

Having made their basic shapes, the children should then be encouraged to decide what sort of person his tube might represent. Does it make him think of a pleasant person, a grouchy person, an old person? When he decides he may proceed to make his puppet. Using cut papers, scissors, and paste, he develops a face. Since this type puppet works best for the middle or upper elementary grades it is a good plan for the teacher to encourage some three-dimensional experimentation with the cut paper on the puppet. Perhaps one child may discover a way to make the lips stick out from the face while another may find a way to make the cheeks bulge, while still another may invent a new type of eyelid or eyelash. Still others may work out ways of making hair, mustaches, whiskers, ears, or tongues. Others may decide to put hats on their puppets. Some may make a bonnet type while others may make hats with large floppy brims, and certainly some boy will make a high silk hat like Uncle Sam always wears. It is a wise teacher who encourages the children to experiment and to deviate from standard methods. It is in these variations and rare innovations that the children use their abilities to the utmost and the craft is beginning to fulfill its most significant purposes.

To complete such a puppet, each child can make a small tube of construction paper which fits snugly over his middle finger. This tube is fastened to the inside wall of the puppet head by means of staples, sticky paper, or glue. When the child slides his hand inside the puppet head with the finger firmly inserted in the smaller tube, the puppet is secure and easily managed. A body can be made of heavy construction paper, oaktag, newspapers or whatever materials are readily accessible. The body should be made bulky in order to conceal the child's arm.

The stage may be the classroom piano or a large table tilted on end or perhaps a large piece of wrapping paper can be stretched across a corner of the room. This type puppet is effective especially when the class is adapting a play from classroom reading. It is good because of the few materials required and ease of making but mainly because the shapes of the heads place such limitations on the interpretation of the characters that the children are unable to copy stereotyped concepts. Imagine the ingenuity it will call forth from each child to make Little Red Riding Hood and the Wolf from cylinders rather than making them in a way in which they have always seen them, thus breaking the stereotypes so often found when familiar characters are used.

A Little Variety Maybe

As a modification of the tube puppet the teacher may wish to use this type of tube at Easter time on which to build an Easter hat. If the tubes are made of 12″ × 18″ paper, most likely the hats that the children make on them will be large enough to slip onto their own heads. It is a very hilarious experience to see 25 or so boys and girls each create his own Easter bonnet on a tube, slip it onto his own head, and conduct an Easter parade before the children of the adjoining room. The children will think of hats which Paris has yet to conceive.

Excellent puppets can be made very rapidly on perfectly flat surfaces. A picnic plate will serve as a good form on which to make the head of a two-dimensional puppet. These can be made using some of the same methods previously described such as fastening the picnic plate to a stick and making a body of construction paper or oaktag. Or simply try to invent finger puppets built on simple tubes and decorated with colored papers and scrap materials.

Don't Eat, Light, or Bounce Them

For a variety with the younger children a teacher may want to use fruits and vegetables as the heads for puppets. For example, a potato with a clothespin inserted to hold it by, would serve as an excellent foundation for starting a puppet. The children can bring in buttons, pins, old costume jewelry which would

These little finger puppets can perform on the edge of a desk with each child playing several roles.

An apple or potato serves as a good beginning for a puppet head. The important thing, however, is what is done after the beginning.

serve as facial parts. Perhaps a clothespin inserted into a shiny red apple with features cut from bits of colored papers and pasted fast. Maybe when the apples are ripe there might be some cornsilk to serve as hair and whiskers or grasses might be gathered from a nearby field to serve this same function. Some bits of cloth or even an old stocking from home will make an excellent dress. Sometimes puppets are made from old light bulbs or rubber balls, using similar methods.

But Use Them

Teachers should take these materials and find a way to make them work rather than to believe there is only one right way. If the teacher can not find a way to make them work, the children surely can and will if given the opportunity to work in the materials. It is important when working with puppets as well as other phases of education to insure that each child has a good measure of success. Failure can become habitual. It is wise for the teacher when embarking upon a project of some duration to begin with some directed suggestions so that each child builds a good basic structure on which to create. The child should learn to listen to directions as well as to be able to follow them. In each craft activity the teacher should be able to find a good balance between directed and creative activities.

A Lively Hand Puppet

In the following described puppet activities the teacher should proceed slowly and see that each child keeps up with directions until the basic structure is complete. This is a three dimensional fist or hand puppet which will serve at any level beyond the third grade and which allows such a range of expression that the poorest student will make a successful puppet while the most gifted child can go as far as his creative abilities allow. In starting such a project the

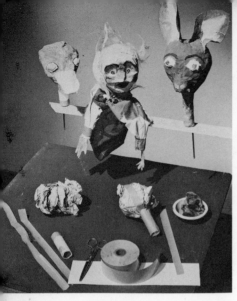

Papier mache puppet heads probably have the greatest range of creative possibilities. These are also very versatile as performers.

materials should be ready to work with so that the class can proceed rapidly and smoothly through the initial stages.

Have prepared for each child a small container with some water in it, a small bundle of newspapers, about one yard of brown sticky paper (gummed kraft tape), a piece of construction paper about three inches wide and about nine inches long, and a pair of scissors. Have the children cut their kraft paper into strips one half inches wide and about one foot long. When this is done take the piece of construction paper and wrap it around the index finger on the hand that the child will use to operate the puppet. This should be wrapped snugly and yet loosely enough that it can be removed easily. Wrap the tube with a piece of gummed kraft paper which has been moistened by a small wad of newspaper that has been dipped into the water. Small bits of kraft tape can be turned over the ends to keep the tube from telescoping when withdrawing the finger. A double sheet of newspaper is then crumpled by starting at one corner and slowly forming it into a ball about the size of a baseball. This is packed like a snowball so that it stays round and compact. One of the foot-long pieces of gummed kraft paper is then moistened and the ball of newspaper placed in the center. The ball is perched on an end of the tube and the free ends of the tape are brought down and stuck onto the tube. This process is repeated with the sticky paper going over different parts of the ball and tube until the ball is firm and secure on top of the tube. A slight wobbling may still be present but will disappear in subsequent steps. A quantity of wallpaper paste is put into the container of each child and his desk is covered with several sheets of newspaper. The children tear pieces of newspaper into small strips which they dip into the paste then apply carefully to the ball and tube. About three coats of these strips are applied to the entire surface. The very slow pupil may not be able to go much beyond this point. But having reached this point he will have a sufficiently good form. Features such as nose, mouth, eyes, and ears can be painted on it. This will be a perfectly satisfactory puppet. This is the point, however, where the real creative part of the puppet making begins.

Now the children must make some decisions regarding their puppets. Who is it or what is it? Will he be kindly or mean, young or old, animal or person, fantastic or realistic? These decisions are easily reached with children. Occasionally the children should make puppets with no special characters in mind. The variety of characters which appear will serve as a stimulation for developing new and interesting stories and plays. Now the major features are built up with larger wads of paper placed wherever necessary. For example: if it is to be a chipmunk with large bulgy cheeks, two wads of paper can be placed in the proper position and fastened down with some strips of newspaper and paste and built up until the cheeks puff out just the way the child thinks they should. From this point on it is a modeling process in which each of the features is built up with small bits of paper soaked in the paste until they are soft and pliable. Some children will add an additional large ball of paper to form a snout or long nose to make an animal such as a pig or goat. Others may cut from 8 or 10 thicknesses of paper large floppy ears for a horse or a hound dog or even ears for a person. These are strengthened by dipping them into the paste so that the edges become saturated and sealed. When the features are completed the puppets are put away to dry.

An occasional performance with both puppets and operators in full view is a good practice. (Courtesy Arts and Activities and Grace Chadwick, Oklahoma City, Okla.)

Put Them Away

There are a number of good ways to dry the puppets. One method is to build a simple rack by drilling holes into a board and inserting short lengths of dowel rods. A simpler rack can be made by pounding large nails into a board and resting each puppet head over a nail. This keeps the forms from being flattened while drying or from sticking to another surface. A convenient method is to suspend them by a string attached to the neck. Hang the heads from the under side of the chalk trough beneath the blackboard. When these have dried overnight they become rigid and hard and have very solid surfaces. They may be worked on in subsequent lessons if necessary but it is important not to allow any of the craft projects to cover too long a period of time, for the interest span of children is limited. Once an interest span has been exceeded it is difficult to continue a project. In the elementary school it takes an exceptionally strong stimulation to hold the interest of children for more than 4 or 5 lesson periods. However, each group is different and teachers may find wide variance in this.

Bring Them to Life

When the heads have dried they are ready to paint. A can of water base or rubber base interior wall paint, makes a good undercoating on which to put the tempera paints and makes the classroom paints go much farther. Certainly one of the children can find a partially used can which he can bring from home. However an undercoat is not essential, and puppet heads can be painted with any kind of paint. If the school budget doesn't provide dry powder paint or tempera paint, the teacher may be surprised by the variety and quantity of paints that the children can bring in from their tool sheds and basements. Naturally the water-based paints are best since no special solvent is necessary to clean the brushes after use.

At the same time the heads are being made the boys and girls can roll tubes to fit the thumb and middle finger. These will serve as the arms and hands of the puppet. There are many ways in which the hands can be made. A simple way is to form a hand of soft thin wire and attach it to the tube, cover the wire with bits of paper and paste. Another method is to cut a hand from a piece of cardboard and fasten it to the tube. If the child wishes he may build the hand up with bits of paper and paste. For some puppets which represent animals the ends of the tubes may be closed with wads of paper and become paws. When the head and hands are completed the children are encouraged to bring in pieces of cloth, old materials, needles, and thread from home to sew a costume. The costume should be made as simple as possible but always large enough so that the hand can easily be inserted inside it, with index finger going into the neck tube and the middle finger and thumb into the hand tubes.

Put Them to Work

Children who make puppets of this type will want to put on performances which require some planning and practice. Simple stages can be made of large cardboard cartons from grocery stores, or a very simple stage can be made by stretching kraft wrapping paper diagonally across a corner of a room. A hole can be cut into the center of it which will serve as the stage opening. A second piece can be stretched similarly, but about 18 inches behind the first. This will serve as the backdrop and on it the children can paint scenery or can make it of colored paper. For a real dramatic performance the room can be darkened and the stage lighted with a spot light or with an ordinary lamp with the light directed into the stage opening. Children old enough to make these puppets should also be inspired to make their own plays. The plays are always more spontaneous if the children are not held rigidly to a script, but rather are permitted to express themselves rather freely within the general ideas or framework of the play. After several practices they will put on a rather polished performance with no script in hand. Puppets of this sort are fine for party days at school or for entertaining parents on special occasions.

A stage can be anything which has an opening and can hide the children who operate the puppets.

Like a Change?

Some teachers prefer to make this type of puppet by first modeling the head from a plastic clay then covering the head with vaseline and building up successive layers of paper and paste until it is about 5 or 6 coats thick. When these layers have dried sufficiently the head is cut in half with a razor blade and the plastic clay removed. Then the edges are sealed together with bits of paper and paste, thus making a very light but strong head with which to work. This method takes a great deal more time and effort than the previously described one and it has a tendency to produce stiffer, less free puppet heads. Where accuracy and detail is desired or is necessary, this method fulfills the need very well.

Momma's Stocking

A very nice type of string puppet can be made from a woman's cotton stocking. This puppet can serve also as a cuddly doll. The children are asked to bring in a stocking from home and some cotton batting or other material suit-

A lady's cotton stocking makes a wonderful puppet—or a doll for a constant companion.

able for stuffing (old nylon hose which has been shredded with scissors), a needle, and some yarn with which to sew. The foot of the stocking is cut off at the ankle leaving just the long tube. The stocking is then turned inside out and one end tied shut with a piece of string. It is turned again right side out. A wad of cotton batting is stuffed into the stocking to form the shape of a head. The stocking is wrapped beneath the head with a piece of yarn or string to form the neck. More batting is stuffed into the stocking to form the upper part of the body. Again the

Marionettes are operated from above by strings attached to the puppets and hung from a simple cross-bar. A child can quickly master enough movements to give them action. (Courtesy Mary Adeline McKibbin, Pittsburgh, Pa.)

56

stocking is wrapped below this to form the waist. Again it is stuffed to form the lower half of the body but this time the child sews across the stocking below the body. With his scissors, the child cuts the remainder of the stocking lengthwise to form the two legs and these in turn are sewn up each side so that they may be stuffed. They are stuffed down to the knee. If there are marbles available, one should be inserted at the knee and the leg wrapped above and below it. This will cause the leg to be flexible and free. If marbles are not available a smooth pebble would serve as well. The rest of the leg is stuffed and the bottom sewed shut. The foot of the stocking is then split lengthwise and the open edges sewed shut to be used as arms. Half of the arm may be stuffed and tied off, a marble or pebble inserted and finished in the same manner as the leg. This will form the elbow joint and make the arm very floppy. The arm is then sewn fast to the shoulder of the puppet. When the second arm is attached, the main part of the puppet is then complete. Bits of felt from old hats may be used to form feet or shoes, bits of light colored cloth may be used for gloves or hands. The feet and hands should be weighted if it is to be used as a puppet. The faces can be made by embroidering the features with yarn or by sewing on buttons or appliqueing pieces of felt or cloth. Hair can be made of pieces of yarn or other scrap material. The puppet can be costumed in whatever manner the child wishes. A search through mother's ragbag will reveal enough interesting pieces of cloth to make adequate costumes for these puppets or dolls. If they are to be used as puppets they are suspended from a crossbar by means of heavy black thread attached at the knees, the shoulders, the hands, and the top of the head. This mechanism should be kept as simple as possible with children so that some motion can be obtained with a minimum of technical know-how.

DRAWING

AND PAINTING

5

DRAWING and painting or picture making can certainly be considered the very backbone of an arts program. However, any program which is limited to just daily drawing with crayons or pencils and occasionally painting a picture with water colors could never be considered adequate to meet the needs of boys and girls. The good program provides a large enough variety of experiences to permit children the opportunity to experiment and to discover new techniques and methods of creating.

Try the Blackboard

When the teacher would like to see her boys and girls truly and intently occupied in a creative process, especially in the lower elementary grades, she might set aside one portion of her blackboard for colored chalk drawing and permit a few youngsters each day to draw on the blackboard. Something about this experience intrigues the children. Perhaps it is the large size of the blackboard or the brilliance of the chalk or the knowledge that what they make can easily be erased or changed (although it seldom is) that opens up new avenues of freedom and permits children the freest sort of self-expression. Here again is an activity where the materials themselves often seem to be stimulating enough to make the children want to draw when given such an opportunity. Some children whose work seems tight and tense in ordinary drawing lessons which use the common drawing or painting materials may find themselves quickly and easily while working on the chalkboard. This, by no means, is a cure-all for children whose work is tight or stereotyped. The good teacher must constantly seek methods or materials which lend themselves to differences in children. No single material or method will ever be adequate to meet the needs of all the children.

When working at the blackboard or chalkboard there are certain small problems of cleanliness that need to be considered. Many of the older schools were not planned with small children in mind. Often you will find all the blackboards in one building at exactly the same height and this height seems to have been determined by the largest children and not by the smaller ones. When this is the case the young children have to reach up over the chalk troughs to work and frequently may soil the sleeves of their dresses or shirts. It is a good plan for the teacher to prepare or to have the mothers of the children prepare simple smocks for "dirty activities." Most parents are eager to help with the activities of the schools and if the mothers are asked to make a smock from one of the father's old shirts she will probably do so. The collar can be removed from the shirt, the sleeves shortened and elastic tape put in the ends of the sleeves to

The chalkboard will always be full of interesting pictures if children are given the opportunity to use it.

make it fit tight at the wrists so that the sleeves may be pulled up above the elbows in such activities as finger painting. Smocks can be worn backwards— that is with the buttons going down the child's back. Decorating the smocks can be an interesting project in itself.

On Colored Paper

Usually a change of materials is very stimulating. Occasionally the children should be given large pieces of colored paper and, if possible, be permitted to choose their own color. The older elementary children and junior and senior high school boys and girls can achieve extremely beautiful results by using colored chalks or pastels. Using large colored paper and soft chalks for outdoor sketching will result in brilliant and beautiful pictures. When doing outdoor sketching, if drawing boards are not available it is easy to obtain a good supply simply by having the children bring in large cardboard cartons and cutting pieces about 18 by 24 inches from them. These are light to handle and much easier to store than wooden drawing boards and are certainly easier for the children to carry for their outdoor work.

Try Wet Paper

If the chalk has a tendency to be dusty and occasionally soils the desk tops and shirt sleeves, the class might try an experiment working with colored chalks and wet paper. If a sink is available and can be filled with water, the paper can be made wet by taking two sheets at one time, holding them together by the corners and submerging them into the water. If this is done quickly the papers can be separated with the inside surfaces still dry and then placed on the desks with the wet side up. However, if a sink is not available, newspapers can be spread out on the desk tops and a small amount of water poured on each child's paper which can be spread with the palm of the hand until the whole surface is wet. While it is wet he begins working with chalk. The moisture holds the dust of the chalk and pulls a great deal of color from the stick, resulting in very brilliant pictures. This is an especially nice way of working when creating free and large designs. If the class enjoys the experience of working on the wet paper they may wish to try some other experiments on wet paper. If stiff brushes such as easel brushes or brushes similar to those used for oil painting and some dry powder paints are available, several children may experiment in this method. Place a small amount of dry powder paint of each color in separate containers such as dry muffin tins or jar lids, moisten a piece of heavy drawing paper or bogus paper, a gray porus drawing paper, and give the child a bristle brush. Have the child moisten the tip of the brush on the wet paper and then dip it into his first color. The dampness of the brush will cause some of the powder paint to adhere to the bristles and when it is wiped across the wet paper the moisture on the paper will cause the dry powder to become liquid paint. On this stroke the brush will pick up enough moisture so that when it is dipped into a second color or back again into the same color it will pick up enough dry paint to make another stroke on the paper. Each time the brush touches the paper it picks up enough moisture to cause the dry powder to adhere. If the paper remains moist enough the whole painting can be completed without having to moisten the brush at any time.

Very rich and unusual effects occur because of the paint fusion which takes place on the wet paper. Sometimes the paintings must dry and the children are permitted to rework certain areas to emphasize parts which, perhaps, blurred more than they had desired or had become softer in color than they wished. Correcting or overpainting is a perfectly permissible practice if it helps the child to express himself more clearly. Processes which permit of free expression of ideas are good processes. Teachers should do away with fears of not doing things the "right" way. The right way is only right in one's own opinion.

Creating Large Paintings

Teachers who work with very small children realize the importance of having large brushes and large materials for easel paintings because of the interest many small children have for filling spaces rapidly. Many types of excellent easel brushes are available to the classroom teacher but sometimes she may wish to create her own oversized brushes by using ordinary paint or enamel brushes from the hardware store. These inexpensive, black bristle brushes can be carefully trimmed so that their bristles are short and firm for easel painting. Another very good practice for large paintings is to cut a cellulose sponge, like those used for household cleaning or car washing, into blocks about one inch square and two to three inches long. Several of these at the easel can supplement your brush supply. The children can be taught to use this sponge effectively for painting. The child can dip one end of the sponge into the paint and quickly fill a whole sky or the color of a dress or a tree without having to continually dip as he must do with a brush. The classroom teacher should not be too disturbed by lack of easels or fancy art equipment. The floor is an excellent place to paint, in many respects better than an easel. Fine paintings can be made on brown

It is natural for small children to work on the floor where they can have unrestricted space and freedom.

wrapping paper, newspapers, dry cleaning bags and on the sides of large cardboard cartons. Even if the class store room is adequately stocked with conventional art materials the teacher ought to try occasionally to bring variety into her program through the use of some of these other materials. An occasional use of unusual materials can be a stimulus for children to look and to conceive of old materials in new ways and can help do away with the idea that good art or creative work can only be done with expensive supplies.

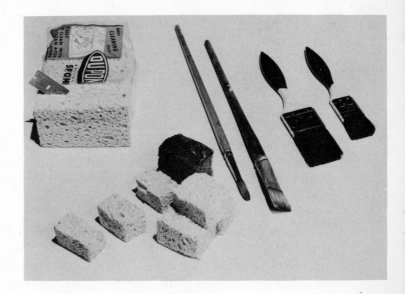

Broad brushes and cellulose sponge-pieces suggest the filling of larger areas which may be neglected with small brushes which require monotonous laboring.

Finger Painting

Finger painting is an activity which is held in very high esteem in some quarters and looked upon as a very unpleasant activity in others. Finger painting lends a certain quality of freedom and release to the art program and it does serve an important function in the ordinary classroom. At some time or another it should be included in every arts and crafts program. Many teachers omit it from their program in the elementary schools for two main reasons. The first is that they believe it is a dirty, messy, noisy experience which leads to confusion or chaos and the second reason is that teachers do not know or understand the medium, therefore omit it. Finger painting can be handled successfully by any teacher in almost any situation. Imagine the most primitive situation in which the classroom is furnished with old fashioned desks, each with its inkwell and a pencil trough, the desks are screwed down to the floor in rigid rows, the tops slant and are too small for pieces of paper. In such a room the teacher must use the floor as the working space. Around the outer edge of the room she can have one of the children place a layer of clean newspapers and on top of the newspapers the child can place sheets of finger painting paper on which to work. The teacher can buy good finger paint from any school supply house or

With a planned approach, finger painting is easy and provides a valuable experience.

she can make excellent finger paint in her own kitchen. To make finger paint a large portion of ordinary laundry starch is prepared similar to the starch normally used for collars and cuffs. However, the proportions are increased so that the starch is considerably thicker than for laundry purposes. For the teacher who is a novice at making starch she might follow these directions:

Mix the dry starch with some cold water until it is a smooth, thin paste, put it in the bottom of a large container like a bucket, boil some water in another container and when it is bubbling lift it from the heat and pour it rapidly into the container holding the starch paste. If it is poured from a rather high position the water goes down rapidly and churns up the starch paste, mixing it quickly and smoothly so that no lumps result. If the water is added slowly, a dribble at a time, it is sure to become lumpy. Once the starch is mixed the teacher can add a small handful of soap flakes or detergent. This will make it very easy for the children to clean their hands at the end of the finger painting experience, or if some should get onto the clothing it will make it easy to clean or to wash out without leaving a stain. If any child should get some finger paint onto his trousers or shirt during the finger painting process the teacher should see that it is allowed to dry until it is hard before doing anything about it. When perfectly dry, it can generally be picked off with the finger nails from the surface of the garment without leaving any stain or mark whatsoever. If the teacher tries to wipe it off while it is wet the colors only rub deeper into the fabric making it more difficult to clean.

When the finger paint paper is in place the children can kneel before it on the clean newspapers and the teacher can go around the room pouring a small pan full of clear starch onto each child's paper. The teacher will quickly learn to judge the amount to pour on each paper. It is not necessary to moisten the papers because there is enough moisture contained in the liquid starch to do the job well. One of the children can follow the teacher sprinkling a small amount of dry powdered paint onto the clear starch. Now the children can begin to work and the motions which they make on their paper will mix the paint and starch into a smooth color. This practice saves paint because if any of the starch is left after the finger painting experience it can be thrown away or stored away for several weeks without spoiling.

The children are encouraged to make large and free motions while painting, using closed fists, open hands, sides of their hands, lower arms, knuckles and all sorts of rhythmic motions. It is a good practice to encourage them to make designs or motions rather than pictures with the finger paint because if they limit their activities to the rigid drawing of pictures the whole value of the finger paint process is lost. With a starch mixture on the finger paint paper the children are able to work for long periods of time changing their designs, wiping out, creating all sorts of new motions, wiping out, and continuing this process. If the paintings become a little sticky and the children wish to continue working longer, simply add a bit more starch. And, finally, when the children feel their paintings are complete they should leave them on the floor, wash their hands and return to their seats, ready for their next class. If no sink is available a bucket of warm, soapy water and a scrubbing brush and some large sheets of newspapers, in the absence of paper towels, on which to dry their hands should be placed somewhere near the center of the room. This will easily solve the clean-up problem. At the first recess the teacher can have one of the children gather the dry paintings, another gather the newspapers which were beneath them. The old newspapers can be destroyed and the paintings displayed.

Often the finger paintings can be used for notebook covers or to cover waste baskets made of old five gallon ice cream cartons. They can be pressed flat with a warm iron and will make interesting displays around the classroom wall. They always look more interesting if they can be matted or carefully mounted on a larger piece of paper. If the finger paint paper is not available or is too expensive for the classroom budget finger paintings can be done with the starch on almost any type of paper, but preferably one with a smooth, non-porous surface. Magazine covers, heavy laundry bags, butcher paper, shelf paper are all good for this activity. Shelf paper is perhaps the most satisfactory of these papers. Most children thoroughly enjoy finger painting activities and will want to repeat this experience many times. Occasionally the feel of finger paint may be repulsive to a child. When this is the case, the teacher is unwise to force the child to continue in such a situation, but rather should permit the child to engage in an activity which is more pleasant to him.

Crayon Resist

Most classrooms are equipped with wax crayons but often they are used in only one way—that is, to make crayon drawings on manilla or white paper. There are a number of good variations which the teacher might try with crayons to enrich or to enliven her program. Occasionally, when the children make a

The wax crayon resists colored water paint while the uncrayoned areas are covered with it, changing a day picture into a night picture.

crayon drawing the teacher may have them work over their drawings in a very heavy manner pressing the wax on as thick as possible and leaving some areas of the drawing entirely free of any crayon. The first such experience might come without the children knowing what is to follow, therefore, is an unplanned experience or drawing. When the drawings have been completed the teacher might suggest that the children mix a small quantity of a dark water color and brush it over the entire surface of the crayon drawing. The dark water color will fill in all areas which the crayon has not covered but will be resisted on all areas that the crayon has covered. This may give the feeling of a night picture or change the entire character of the drawing which the child has made suggesting other things which might follow. Now a second drawing might be made in which the child definitely plans "it is night" or "on the stage of the theatre" or "in the dark circus tent" or "at the ice follies" or some other similar situation in which the major portions are darkened and certain areas are emphasized. Now he makes his drawing with crayons consciously planning what is going to happen when the water color or, in some cases, ink is washed across it. It is a thrilling experience to see the change which transpires when the water color crosses the surface of the paper. It is this sort of experience which enriches the program and causes the child to project and to imagine in ways in which he had not done so before.

Crayon Etching

Another crayon technique is the crayon etching which again can be done in a similar manner. This technique is most successful if carried out on very smooth paper or on a piece of oak tag. Each child is given a piece of paper or oak tag perhaps 5″ × 7″ or 6″ × 8″ or 6″ × 9″ and permitted to take any of the bright colors from his crayon box and begin to cover the entire surface of the paper putting one color here and another color there occasionally blending two colors together until the whole surface is entirely covered with bright colors. When this

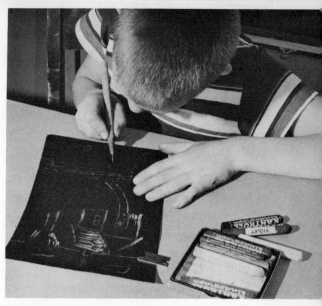

Some children desire to show careful detail in their pictures. The crayon etching or scratchboard technique is well suited for fine detail.

is done the child selects his black crayon and puts a surface coating of black crayon all over the top of the other colors. If any ink is available this step can be done with India ink instead of waxed crayon. When the top has been entirely blackened the child begins to make his picture by scratching through the top layer exposing the colors which lie beneath the surface, using the pointed tip of a compass or an old pen point. The tip of a pocket knife or any other similar, sharp, pointed instrument will serve as a scratching tool. This particular tool intrigues the children who are interested in minute detail and great accuracy, for here they can develop intricate drawings with the point of a pen or scratching tool. Some children are probably bothered by the fact that they cannot get rich detail when they are always compelled to use large, blunt crayons for drawing. The teacher should be aware of the need for such a variety of experiences which give opportunity for each type of child to find himself in one medium or another.

Crayon Encaustics

The classroom teacher may find that she is gathering many small bits of various colored pieces of broken crayon which seem to accumulate until great quantities are available. Crayon encaustic will help dispose of these bits. Drop bits of each color into the six or eight depressions of an old muffin tin keeping

Crayon encaustic is limited to individual rather than class projects. A heavy cardboard or piece of plywood makes a good painting surface.

67

all the reds in one, all the blues in another, all the greens in a third, and so on. Melt these crayons over a hot plate until they are in a liquid form. The top of the hot plate could be covered with a piece of aluminum foil to prevent drippings of the melted crayon from soiling the hot plate and falling into the coils and smoking. While these crayons are in a melted or liquid form they can be used in the same way oil and oil painting would be done. Stiff bristle brushes are far superior to hair brushes for this process. The wax cools and dries very rapidly when it is removed from the muffin tin so that children must learn to work exceedingly fast and freely. Because of the speed in working the pictures become brilliant and fresh and display new techniques not seen in any other medium. Because this requires a certain speed and dexterity this is a project which works best in the junior and senior high schools. After the paintings are covered additional experiments can be conducted by the children by adding additional heat to the surface of the painting with a small alcohol torch causing additional fusing of color. This type of painting can be done on practically any surface. Old posters or old pieces of cardboard, scraps of masonite, cardboard boxes are all good surfaces on which to work. The completed paintings done with this hot wax method can be given additional interest by using some of the scratch methods described in the earlier crayon etching process.

Ordinary Water Colors

Often in our schools we find many boys and girls who have lost confidence in their ability to create. This loss of confidence generally occurs when there is a discrepancy between what the child can produce and what the child wishes he could produce. In other words, his technical skills have not caught up to his mental maturity or his conscious awareness and when this condition exists it is important for the arts and crafts teacher to find methods which will help the child regain confidence in his own ability to create, to permit him to make drawings or paintings or crafts which will satisfy his critical nature. This period of development generally occurs in the upper elementary grades, the junior high school and sometimes in the senior high school. One of the methods to use to help boys and girls who are at this stage of development regain confidence in themselves is the accidental water color. The child is given a large piece of drawing paper which he moistens with water until it is well saturated on its drawing surface and then the teacher may say, "Today we are going to do some water color experiments. We are going to try to create some moods with our water colors and the first mood we will make will be a pleasant and happy mood. Now, think of some colors which come to your mind when you think of a happy situation. What would they be? They could be red, yellow, pink or green. Well, you decide which of these colors would be your happy colors. Moisten each of these colors in your water color box and when they are all wet pick up a color with your brush and put it on to your drawing paper in any fashion you want, then move on to the next color and put it on to the paper being careful never to cover any color which has been placed on before. Continue this until your whole paper is covered with bright colors showing a happy mood."

In doing this the colors will fuse in very unusual ways covering the whole surface and creating all sorts of brilliant accidents. While this paper is drying the teacher may ask them to think up another mood, perhaps an unpleasant mood, and then to think of all the colors which seem unpleasant to them. This time they may use dark colors such as black, purple, dark greys and browns and again cover the entire surface with colors that they think of as unpleasant. On this exercise the teacher may wish to have the paper even wetter than on the first experience thus creating entirely different sorts of fusions. If large puddles remain, these can be easily blotted up with the tip of the brush or with an ink blotter. The teacher should exercise caution to see that the children do not pick up their paintings while wet to show them to one another thus causing all the colors to fuse into a kind of homogenized grey. Rather, she should encourage them to allow the pictures to lie flat until perfectly dry.

On the next lesson the class may choose their first water color and the teacher may talk about this as though it were a sky which they saw one bright, sunny morning while walking out across fields, and as they walked they came to a hill. They looked up over the hill and there they saw some things, perhaps a barn or a tree or a house or an animal or a farmer at work. The children will begin to suggest what they may have seen on the top of the hill. Now on the surface of the bright water color sky they are permitted to sketch the hill and the things they imagine they have seen. From this point on the hill, the things which stand

Creative work requires intense concentration and careful thought the same as any other important work. Although it is enjoyable, it is not play.

on the top of it are painted on opaquely with black water color or with India ink. The opaque foreground contrasts against the brilliance of the transparent background gives a very dramatic effect. Each child, regardless of the simplicity of his work, creates a rather startling picture which will have a mature appearance. The second paper may be used to have the children sketch at their homes the things they see silhouetted against the sky in the evening. This can be painted onto the water color sky with black water color or with India ink. Other pictures may be made of skylines or shorelines or just shores or even to create the illusion of a body of water. The best subject matter is always derived from the experiences of the children. Any teacher will realize that this is a limiting process which is not as free as one would normally desire in a classroom but when the class is filled with children who are unwilling or unable to create, the teacher must do some things in order to start them working. This particular procedure does much to help them regain their confidence. After several lessons of this sort the children are generally ready and willing to try things which are new and are different. Through such an experience the children may gain confidence in their teacher and regain confidence in themselves. From this point on teaching becomes a much more pleasant and rewarding experience.

The same procedure could be used with tempera paints if water colors are not available. The tempera paints have a more opaque quality but are very rich and lend themselves better to over-painting. If both water colors and tempera paints are available in the classroom the teacher may begin with the transparent water colors on an opaque foreground and move on into using tempera paints on wet paper. But instead of using a black opaque foreground, permit the children now to use whatever colors they desire to paint in the foreground. In this manner she may work in the direction of the free, more expressive paintings which she normally would desire.

Try a Piece of Window Glass

Most of the drawings which boys and girls make in the classroom end up mounted or matted and they are hung on the wall or on the bulletin board. Occasionally, for variety, the teacher may wish to make a stand-up picture which may have greater interest and more brilliance than a picture hanging on the bulletin board. A piece of square window glass and a short length of 2×4 lumber which has been notched to hold the glass are all that are needed for a stand up picture. Using any paints which will adhere to glass and which have a transparent quality, the children can paint stand up pictures to be placed in front of windows. The light passes through the pictures and creates the feeling of a stained glass window. There are some excellent paints available to the classroom teacher for this sort of activity from most school supply houses. However, a very adequate substitute can be made by adding a sufficient quantity of clear varnish to colored enamels to render the enamels translucent, if not transparent.

And in Conclusion

There are many, many other ways of painting in the classroom and as is the case with all phases of the art program, the classroom teacher must use the materials she has available and to try to use them sometimes in ways different from standard practices. It is important to be experimental and to try ways others have not tried before you. But it is not a good idea to turn one's back upon good standard practices. Some teachers feel that to use any method which has been tried before or used successfully by others is a poor thing to do. This is an attitude which is ridiculous and pure folly.

Often teachers ask, "What is the right way to use water colors? What is the right way to use crayons?" Answer: there is no right way or wrong way, so long as the materials are used in such a way that the children have the opportunity to express themselves in their own manner. Children are like great painters: they develop their own personal techniques through working and not through listening.

SEASONAL ACTIVITIES

AND THE HOLIDAYS

6

ART WORK for special days or special occasions sometimes brings out the very best in our classes but at other times it can be an opportunity for the very worst kind of art work. Some of the richest experiences and deepest feelings which children have are experienced at the holiday seasons or during special events. We know, for example, of the special motivation most children feel during the Christmas season when stores, homes and religious institutions, as well as the school and the individual classroom are overflowing with the feeling and the beauty of Christmas. Unfortunately some schools do not make the most of these rich experiences, but rather use this time to pass out patterns and decorate the schools with the poorest kinds of stereotyped materials. Walls and windows are filled with row upon row of Santa heads or snowmen, each exactly like the one next to it. Generally these patterns are examples of the poorest kind of art activities, almost devoid of the real meaning of the season which the child is experiencing. Some schools discourage or prohibit the teaching of religious subjects on school time, but many have no objection to an objective examination of the religious holidays and special events of all religions.

Mural Making

The making of large group murals provides an excellent outlet for the feelings of special seasons and special holidays and develops within the children a spirit for working together, an understanding of the problems of their classmates, and learning to give and take in a good manner.

Imagine a classroom of fourth grade children who want to make a large mural on brown wrapping paper to cover the blackboard for the impending Christmas and Hanukkah seasons. Through discussion with the group perhaps the topic "Our Town During the December Holidays" could be selected as a topic. Now the teacher may suggest, "Let us write on the board everything that we know about our town before we begin. How many parts are there to our town?" she might ask. Back come the answers, "There is the business section, there is a residential section, there is a factory section, there is a farming section," and so on. If any major sections of town have been omitted the teacher might suggest them or may, through additional questions, draw out the needed answers. By now the main headings have been written on the blackboard. Now the teacher might ask, "What kind of buildings would we find in the business section?" and back come answers such as "Banks and stores and hotels, theatres," and so forth. Then the teacher may wish to inquire deeper into this. "What special stores do you think of?" Some say, "The dime store and the candy store and the toy store

The meaning of cooperation is best learned through a cooperative project such as a cut-paper mural.

and the gift store, the department store," and so on. Moving on to the residential section the teacher might ask, "What kind of buildings could we find here?" and back come answers, "Houses and apartments and churches and garages." Through additional questioning the teacher may find more about the type of houses. "What kind of houses do we live in in this town?" and again the replies come back, "Wood houses and brick houses and big houses, small houses and double houses, old houses, new houses." By continuing this process through all the main sections, the board will soon be filled with the things that the children know about their own community. Then the teacher might ask, "What makes our community different at the holiday season from any other season?" Some child will suggest snow and colored lights and decorations and Christmas trees and many people shopping and bundles, and so on, and one child might say, "Let's make it like night so the lights will show." Finally, when all the facts have been written on the board the teacher might suggest they begin. "How shall we begin?" she asks. "Let each of us do a part," a child may suggest. She may ask each child to select one thing that he wants to make and checks it off as it is chosen. After each child has chosen the thing he wants to make and begins to assemble it with cut paper and paste the teacher can select two or three children to prepare a background either with tempera paint, chalk, or with colored paper, working directly on the brown wrapping paper which by now has been fastened on to the wall.

It is not necessary or even good to have a preconceived idea of how this might turn out, for as the children begin to work on the background the ideas will flow freely. They will be able to adequately solve the problems without much assistance from the teacher. Meanwhile, at their seats the children are working along, some rapidly and some more slowly, and when the ones who have finished first come to the teacher and say, "I am all finished," then the teacher can suggest, "What other important things have we omitted?" or "Suppose you start making people" or "Suppose you start making trees" or "Suppose you start making strings of lights or automobiles." There are a multitude of small details which always need to be filled in at the end and by holding some of these back it keeps a good balance on the use of class time so that all children are working all the time. Finally, when everyone has completed his task, including the small details, the group can stop, put the work aside to discuss the organization of the mural. Now the teacher might ask, "What shall we put in the center of our mural?" and a child might answer, "Let us put the business center in the center of our mural," so, one by one, the business buildings are brought up by the children and pinned to the background in a temporary manner. Next, perhaps, the residential buildings, and finally the factories and industrial areas, and beyond that the farming buildings if this happens to be the sequence in which they would be found. Now comes the matter for discussion and understanding. Most likely there will be too many objects for each to be seen in its entirety so the problems of overlapping will begin. There may be an unbalance or poor distribution which the children will want to correct when they see the mural parts all assembled. Through these overlappings in cut paper the children begin to understand the meaning of overlapping in drawing and painting. Surely through the discussion the children will say they need more of this or more of that and all their remarks are kept in mind and later some children can volunteer to make the needed parts. Finally, when it is concluded that the group has developed the best possible arrangement with the added parts, the whole mural is pasted into place. In the end the children will experience a great delight for what they have accomplished as a group. The real meaning and value of group activity will be felt in each of them. Each child will realize that what the group has done together he could not have done by himself. The poorest student can identify with this mural and say, "It is part mine," and get the deep sense of accomplishment he needs to feel. This mural procedure is simply one of dozens and dozens of procedures which can be used.

Mural-making fits any age group and usually is an effective group project for special events or for the culmination of a unit of study.

The same method could be used by drawing or painting individual pictures, cutting them out and pasting them on a background, or by having each child paint over a longer span of time a part directly on a large mural. It is unreasonable to think that one method is better than another. The teacher simply must make the decision as to what method will work best in her room, her group's age level, and the conditions under which she must work.

Peep Shows

There is always an air of excitement and enthusiasm in the room when the children are making peep shows. Pupils in all grades enjoy creating with boxes. A good type of box for a peep show is a shoe box. Most any shoe store will be glad to provide a sufficient number of boxes for the average class at most any time. A good peep show requires some imagination in the selection of scrap materials to make it, and a good solid motivation so that they are not trite or stereotyped. Generally enough materials can be gathered from a school yard— weeds, twigs, sawdust from the shop, pebbles, stones, leaves, vines, cotton, bits of stick, and as many other scrap materials as one can find for developing the peep shows. At one end of the box a hole about the size of a quarter or fifty-cent piece is cut with a pair of scissors and the top is opened at the opposite end to permit light to enter. Sometimes, for variety, holes are also placed on both sides to give a kind of spot light or theatre lighting effect. Now, on the inside bottom of the box the scene is built. Perhaps it will be a summer rodeo or a winter ice skating scene.

From scrap material available the children will soon conceive of uses for the various materials which it includes. A bit of broken mirror becomes a skating pond,

The peep-show is full of surprises because it challenges the ingenuity of each child to invent new uses for his collection of materials.

broken twigs a camp fire and crumpled cellophane the fire itself, colored papers the mountains in the background, and bits of cotton hung on thread clouds floating overhead, and a twig stuck in a piece of modeling clay becomes a tree, and little figures are modeled from plasticine or pipe cleaners. Here a stone may be a boulder and a bit of sand a mountain trail, and a chestnut burr becomes a porcupine, and so it goes with children finding new and imaginative uses for otherwise useless or scrap materials. This is the creative process in action. Finally, with colored cellophanes covering some of the openings in the box, the child can light his peep show just as a stage designer lights his set making a hole or an opening larger or perhaps closing one of the openings, changing from a yellow piece of cellophane to a clear piece or a blue piece, thinking, changing, deciding, a constant flow of problems and solutions, a constant flow of ideas and thoughts. This is the value of crafts in elementary education. At last comes the thrill when each child gets to peep into the opening of his neighbor's peep show, and allows his to be viewed by others. With all of them placed on the window ledges the children can go around the room getting a new pleasure and excitement each time he peers into a new peep show.

Dioramas

The peep show process can be used in a large box with slight modifications by opening a whole side or by simply not using the lid of the box and standing it on its side. The scene can be constructed and the side or top opening covered with a piece of colored cellophane or clear cellophane. To do this provides a psychological barrier between the viewer and the scene and gives the feeling of looking into another world. This diorama makes a fine group project in the same

What started as a lesson in salt ceramic modeling ended as a circus complete to the last spectator.

way that a cut paper mural provides a good group project. In the study of a unit on Mexico, Australia, your community, a farm, or an airport, the children might wish to construct a diorama or a model to culminate all their thinking, learning, and research which has taken place during the study of the unit. Perhaps this time larger figures can be modeled, using the salt ceramic formula which is given in the chapter on Modeling and Sculpture in this book. Such activities enrich any learning situation and give the children a deeper feeling of identification with things that they study and all this goes to make a happier, more useful school situation.

Candle Making

This project has limited creative possibilities because it allows little opportunity for individual differences. However, it is not a detrimental activity, and it can add some glamour to learning Christmas songs. Almost every household magazine has descriptions of fancy and interesting candles for the Christmas season in their November and December issues, but one procedure not described which is most useful for very small children in the elementary school is as follows. During the fall season the teacher encourages children to bring in broken or partially used candles, which have been discarded, until a sizable quantity has been gathered. An SOS to the PTA will aways be answered with a good supply. On the day that the teacher chooses to make the candles she will need to have a hot-plate to melt down the old candles and several large containers like #10 cans to melt them in. The candles are slowly melted until they are entirely in a liquid state, using all care to avoid unnecessary dangers of spilling. Wicks should be prepared in advance by cutting about foot-long pieces of heavy cotton cord and dipping these once into hot wax so that they have an initial stiffness and straightness. When the wax is prepared it can be placed in two #10 cans, one at each end of the room, in positions that are safe and cannot tip over. The cans of wax can be placed inside small cardboard cartons. Now the teacher may combine the singing of some Christmas or winter songs with the making of the candles. The children gather around the perimeter of the room, each with a wick in his hand, and the singing begins, and as the children sing their Christmas songs they walk around the room and each time they pass the wax they dip the wick into the hot wax, lift it out, and continue their walk around the room. By the time they have reached the second can of wax the candle will have cooled sufficiently to go into the warm wax again. This is a much better way than dipping back and forth from the warm wax into cold water. In the water-wax method droplets of water are imbedded in the hot wax and all during the burning process they pop and sizzle and sometimes actually extinguish the wick. A dozen or so trips around the room singing will provide each child with a very large and attractive candle which will burn well and which will be personal to the child. This could provide a useful yet simple present for one of the parents

Stubs of old candles plus some paraffin and wax crayons melted together can be remade into holiday candles.

at Christmas time. Bits of broken crayons can be dropped into the wax during the melting process to give beautiful bright colors to the candles.

The problem of Christmas gift-giving is one of the major sore spots in craft and art education. Many schools through precedent have established the annual gift-giving routine and teachers are plagued with the problem of making something new or different. Invariably these gifts end up being little gimcracks or gadgets which do not truly express the creativeness of children or the spirit of the holiday but only satisfy the need for a Christmas gift to give. The teacher should slowly work around this problem so that if the gift-giving must continue, the things which are given have meaning to the child as well as to the parent and the teacher.

Cookie Decoration

Many special events or occasions call for small parties or treats at the school, and cookies may be needed. For these parties the teacher can have the children or their parents bring in plain, undecorated cookies. The children can have an

Each cookie becomes the child's work of art before it reaches the party table.

79

interesting art or craft lesson decorating the cookies for the party. All that is needed are some clean paper cups, a box of confectioners sugar, a small quantity of milk, and some vegetable dyes. It is a good idea to mix one large cup of powdered sugar and sufficient milk to attain an "icing" consistency. The teacher could do this perhaps in a cup or a bowl with a fork or spoon then place some in each of the paper cups to which several drops of vegetable dye can be added. This can be stirred up with a spoon or tongue depressor and the children then may paint with the icing their designs on the cookies, using tooth picks or paste sticks as the painting instrument. There is no need to tell the children how to decorate a cookie for they will come forth with the most imaginative and most beautiful cookies one has ever seen and mothers, fathers, and guests will be surprised and happy to see the designs they get to eat. The occasion may suggest the types of designs that the children create.

Decorations

On some occasions in the classroom the children may desire to decorate the room for a party or a "fair" or at Christmas to decorate a tree. Every teacher knows that there are limitless possibilities in creating interesting and original decorations. While lots of patterns for making decorations are available decorations are meaningless to the child unless he has a part in designing them. Even though it may sometimes be difficult to do, teachers and parents should constantly think of the activities of the classroom in terms of the values of them to the children. The child should never be secondary to the product he makes. This is not to imply, however, that the product is of no value or importance, for the product is always a record of the child's experience. If it is a deep experience and if the child is sufficiently motivated through the experience the product will invariably be a good one if measured by standards of childhood development

Paper scraps are easily reshaped, bent, folded or combined, then strung on thread as party decorations.

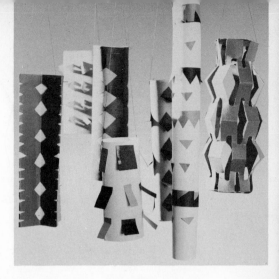

Old "Japanese lanterns" of yesteryear can be creative if approached without patterns or preconceived plans. They will brighten a dull corner for the class party.

rather than by adult standards. If the experience is shallow or weak the product will have little feeling and it will have little meaning to the child who makes it.

Chicken Egg

Eggs are used in almost every household and are, therefore, a very ready material for craft work. The trick, however, is to use the eggs without breaking the shells. This can be done by penetrating each end of the egg with a small hole and blowing out the content. This makes fine scrambled eggs but will not do, of course, if father likes his eggs served sunny side up. There are always enough interested parents who will try to save hollow egg shells for certain classroom activities. In some instances hard boiled eggs will serve just as well. The eggs can be beautifully decorated with tempera paints or with wax crayons or with glue and glitter, cut paper or metallic paper pasted on to them or simply with water colors. These when hung by a thread from a tree make most beautiful Christmas balls. Another good project with eggs, and these can be hard boiled ones, is to use them at Easter time to make pretty little ladies' heads wearing Easter

Some crayons, paints or bits of colored paper and glitter can make yesterday's breakfast into tomorrow's tree trimming.

The egg-head may not rate high in politics but it can be tops as a party favor. (Courtesy Arts and Activities and Elizabeth Stein, Bloomington, Ill.)

bonnets. A simple collar can be made of a strip of construction paper, large enough to hold the egg so that it sits solidly. Faces can be developed with paints or colored papers, colored pencils, colored scrap materials; finally, each child might design a beautiful Easter bonnet to sit on top of the head. By this time the children will also be thinking of ways to make hair, collars, scarfs, bows, and so on. This can also serve as an interesting fashion project. Actually, the eggs can be used for a multitude of small figures, for the egg shape may suggest birds, fish, animals, insects, rocket ships, in fact, anything which remotely resembles the oval form. While you work with the egg you should also consider the many possibilities of the egg carton and how the interesting pressed shapes of the pulpy paper dividers lend themselves to a variety of uses.

Salt Ceramic Again

The salt and corn starch which is described in the chapter on Modeling and Sculpture lends itself well to making tree ornaments or decorations. Among the simplest forms will be little balls which the children could roll in the palms of their hands and pinch into them a bit of string which will dry in place and can be used for hanging. These, when dry, can be decorated with paints or glitter; smaller ones can be rolled and a match stick pushed through the center of them to form beads of all sizes, shapes, and varieties, and these, when painted and strung, make beautiful hangings for the elementary school Christmas tree. Some-

Even the youngest children can shape
and paint their own tree decorations.
Salt ceramic can be manipulated
similarly to clay.

times the salt ceramic can be pressed out flat like pie dough and with a dull paring knife the children can cut out shapes in the same way they would cut out Christmas cookies, and a bit of string stuck into it while wet will serve as the hanging device. When dry these can be painted on both sides and decorated as the children desire. Small figures, birds, butterflies, insects, and geometric shapes would be interesting to make from the salt ceramic to place on a tree or to use as room decorations. A little soft wire stuck into the bottom of the bird before it dries would serve to wrap around a tree branch to hold the bird in place, or a short length of string stuck in its back before it dries would help it to fly when hung overhead in the room. While modeling and sculpturing were discussed fully in another chapter it might be suggested at this point that the salt ceramic lends itself excellently to the making of crèches, Santa's reindeer, carolers, and other modeled figures. Most of the projects described in this section on "Salt Ceramic" could also be made using the papier mache pulp described in the section on Papier Mache and Mask Making.

Balloons and String

A fascinating three-dimensional construction can be made using only a balloon, string, and wallpaper paste or liquid starch. The balloon is inflated to the size

Some children will exercise painstaking care to create highly personal volume-designs over balloons while others wrap them spontaneously.

83

desired and wrapped with string and yarns which are saturated with starch or wallpaper paste. A very clean and good device to use if making a quantity of these is as follows.

Roll your string or yarn into a ball so that it can be unrolled with one continuous pull on the end. Using mayonnaise or pickle jars with screw top lids, fill the jar two thirds full of starch which is smooth and well mixed, punch a small hole in the top of the lid large enough to allow the yarn, string, or thread to pass through it. Place the ball or roll of yarn into the starch or paste, guide the string or yarn through the hole, screw on the lid, and you are ready to start to cover the balloon. Now the string can be pulled out moist in one continuous strand and wrapped around and around the balloon until a sufficient quantity has been placed on to the balloon. Then you can switch to a second color which is in another jar and then a third. This method in the classroom eliminates the messiness of pans of paste and drippy strings all over the place. When these are dry the strings are rigid and strong, the balloon can be punctured, deflated, and gently pulled out from the webbing of strings, leaving a hollow, light, interesting form. This can be enriched with bits of cellophane added here and there, bits of color, sequins, glitter; or they may be left undecorated just as they come off which is a very handsome form in itself. Some teachers prefer to use plaster of paris instead of the paste; however, in the elementary classroom plaster is a bit difficult to use because of the rapidity in drying and the dirtiness of it. Plaster can be slowed down considerably by the addition of a teaspoon of vinegar to about one pound of freshly prepared plaster.

Paste and String

Using the same device as previously described for balloons and string the teacher of very small children can make nice two-dimensional forms by having the youngsters make string forms on waxed paper. These, when dry, form attractive, light weight decorations. The children may wish to make representational decorations using this process and this is desirable.

Broken Glass

Most elementary teachers will shudder at the very notion of bringing broken glass into the classroom. However, there are types of glass which are available which add great glamour to the Christmas tree. A visit to the local hardware store or lumber yard will convince you that almost daily a small barrel full of strips of clear window glass is being thrown away. These bits of glass are in a variety of widths and lengths and could be acquired for decorating with colored enamels or with commercial art paints which are available for use on glass and non-porous surfaces. If the teacher exercises care and caution and adequately instructs her pupils on the handling of the glass there should be no difficulty or nicked fingers.

These bits of glass can be beautifully painted and decorated by the children, allowed to dry. Hangers are made from small pieces of brown gummed tape and the pieces hung here and there through a Christmas tree by thin nylon or silk threads which are long enough to allow some swinging, turning movement of the pieces. These will sparkle and shine and add beauty and life to the dullest tree. Some of these pieces will be large enough to be used for stand up paintings such as described in the chapter on Drawing and Painting.

Banners and Flags

One seldom sees banners and flags being used as an art form in the elementary classroom and yet this particular project is one of the most exciting and enjoyable which the children can do. With the very smallest children a class period of making marching flags is most rewarding. Using thin strips of wood acquired from the scrap boxes of the school shops or the local lumber yards and rectangles of brown wrapping paper as the basis, each child can design his own personal flag using paints or crayons, colored papers, or the materials which are normally found in our scrap boxes in the classroom. However, on certain seasonal or holiday occasions the entire room could be decked in flags and banners representing the occasion being celebrated and here the real meaning of the occasion can be stressed and each child can express in his own way the meaning of that particular holiday or season in a long flowing banner made of brown wrapping paper or shelving paper or ordinary white paper. One end of the banner can be attached to a strip of wood by means of staple or glue and the banner hung from the classroom ceiling or hung from wires stretched from wall to wall. The banner is a device used universally for creating atmospheres or moods for special parades, celebrations, or special days. It is sometimes used in religious rites and ceremonies. Why not try it in the elementary classroom for a gay and cheerful experience?

To parade with one's own flag or banner is a delightful experience and to decorate with them adds charm to any room.

Classroom Windows

For many years the windows of our classroom schools have been used for displaying art works. Unfortunately, most often they were and are still used to display patterns of pumpkins, turkeys or Santa heads but occasionally they are used at Christmas time for large stained glass windows. The use of the classroom window is a good idea but should not be used only to display patterns or to copy or to imitate windows of great churches. Rather the teacher should allow the children to conceive of original, personal uses for this large space. There are excellent paints available now which flow on to glass very easily and are easily washed away. These would do to make large paintings on the windows. Some windows may be covered with thin, white tissue or tracing paper and beautiful designs or pictures made of transparent cellophane or paint applied to these areas. Occasionally, if the windows are of small panes, each child may be assigned a single pane to consider and plan a design for it. Perhaps the use of black construction paper with areas or portions cut out and bits of transparent papers and cellophanes inserted in the open areas would be a solution to the problem. Here again the teacher knows the limits of her own situation. Some may find that the application of designs made of cut paper and paste applied by means of Scotch tape is the only solution while others may find that the administration of their schools encourages the use of the windows for painting and decorating. When this is the case the teacher should utilize every opportunity to display the work of her children to the public who pass by every day.

Three religious scenes are displayed together as the children prepare exhibits of papier maches showing a Mexican Christmas, Hanukkah, and the Nativity. (Courtesy Arts and Activities and Helen Copley Gordon, Detroit, Mich.)

Odds and Ends

The types and kinds of activities that one can engage in during special seasons and holidays is limitless. We can make adaptations of our valentines using many of the procedures described in this book, and almost any occasion might call for a card or a place mat or a special type of decoration. A good discussion with the boys and girls in the classroom will solve many of the problems for the teacher. A simple question, "What do you think we could do for Thanksgiving or Veterans day or Washington's Birthday?" will bring forth a large variety of responses from the children, especially if the teacher creates a climate for free and original thinking. Each special occasion and the special day ought to challenge us in such a way that our programs become richer each year and that our projects become more personal, more individual, more meaningful each time one is tried.

PAPIER MACHE WORK

7

AWHOLE NEW world of experiences can be opened up in any classroom through the medium of papier mache. Unfortunately, papier mache has gained a reputation similar to that of finger paint in that many teachers consider it a dirty, messy experience. But those teachers who have worked in papier mache and have organized their procedures have found it one of the most versatile mediums for use in classroom art work. The only limitations which seem to be placed upon papier mache are placed by one's ability to conceive of new and different uses. For successful experiences in papier mache the teacher needs only the barest minimum of equipment and supplies. Quantities of discarded newspapers, a flour paste, and some bits of string or wire are all that are needed. Many finished papier mache projects are painted with ordinary water based paints but highly successful finishes can be obtained by covering the papier mache with colored paper, cotton, shredded burlap, or any other suitable material which may create an interesting surface texture.

Perhaps the most important thing to think about in conducting a project of papier mache is the method to be used. Actually there is very little confusion or dirt if the teacher takes sufficient time in the beginning to plan a procedure to fit her classroom. If the teacher thinks through the project from the beginning to the end planning each bit of material which needs to be used by the children and has these so organized that the distribution requires a minimum of confusion and moving about in the classroom, she will find that papier mache is a fairly easy medium to use. Imagine, for instance, a fifth grade class of about 30 pupils in an ordinary classroom situation. The group had planned to make a large farm and each child was interested in making a domestic farm animal for the farm. Through advanced planning the teacher and the children had decided upon the size they would make each of these animals and so on the day on which the project is to begin the teacher has ready an adequate quantity of newspapers. Perhaps these are going to be small animals about eight inches long and five to eight inches high. The newspapers have been carefully cut in half so that the sheets are about twelve by sixteen inches. A large container such as a bucket is filled with paste that has been prepared using wallpaper paste flour. This process is easy if the water is placed in the bucket first and the wallpaper flour is sifted slowly into the water and stirred vigorously. By adding the powder to the water it is very easy to get the paste smooth and of the proper consistency. Wallpaper paste can be purchased from any hardware or school supply store. Also ready are about three lengths of wire for each child, each about twelve inches long. If the teacher is in a rural community, she will find many youngsters who can supply her with baling wire, or newsboys from her classes can provide

The finishing touches add much to highly individualized papier mache creatures.

good quantities of wire from their news bundles. It is no trick to get boys from the class to have all the wire prepared and ready to go. In addition there should be a pan at each desk to contain a small quantity of wallpaper paste, several short lengths of string about eight to ten inches long, and if possible about six pieces of sticky paper of the type which is used for wrapping bundles or packages, each about six inches long. Now the teacher provides a sheet of newspaper for each child to cover his desk with and another child distributes half sheets of newspaper, providing each child with about a half dozen sheets. Another child passes the sticky paper, another the string and the wire, and the class is ready to begin. The teacher begins with her instructions and the children follow along step by step.

Paper Coils and Wire

Because of the wide diversification of interests and abilities within every class, the teacher might begin with a basic shape from which each child may later depart in his own direction. Here, as in most crafts, it is essential that the teacher provide the children with a sound foundation or structure in order that every child will have a strong skeleton on which to build. In this case she might ask each of the children to follow along as she describes the process of preparing an "animal" framework. First each child takes a piece of the wire and places it across the twelve inch direction of several sheets of the twelve by sixteen inch newspaper and begins to make a tight roll and when each child has a good solid roll the teacher instructs them to use some of their sticky tape and wrap around each end so that it does not become unrolled. This process is repeated until all three coils are complete. Now two of the coils are bent double to form pairs of legs. Because of the wire inside they will retain their shape. One pair of legs is slipped over the third coil and fastened in place by bits of string or additional sticky paper or even a small bit of wire. When this is firm the second set is placed. Here the child makes the decision. If it is going to be a long, slender bodied animal like a dachshund the legs are placed far apart, if it is to be a tall delicate animal like a calf or fawn the legs are placed close together. When both sets of legs are firmly attached to the third coil, certain decisions must be made by the children. Will this be an animal with a long neck or with a short neck? Will this animal have a bulky or a light frame? Can it be put in a seated position or must it stand? Can the legs be bent to create an illusion of motion or action? Because of the wire inside of the coil the children can modify the positions and shapes considerably at this time. Having made their decision, now they are encouraged to go on forming additional coils for long necks or heads, wadding up additional paper and tying it on to give a full round body, forming a ball as one would for a snow ball, and attaching this by means of the sticky paper. Some children may decide that one set of the legs might better be made wings and may wish to remove one set and reverse their position. Now the process is in the hands of the children and the teacher can only encourage children individually. She should urge each child to experiment to seek ways of solving his problems that are his own ways.

Occasionally the teacher may see an opportunity to make a specific suggestion to an individual child and should capitalize on this opportunity for individual instruction. The gifted children will see a multitude of possibilities and will develop their animals in ways which the teacher never dreamed of, while the slower children may find it difficult to think much beyond the basic structure and may gain their creative satisfaction from painting or decorating this simple form.

When the forms have been developed as fully as possible by adding wads, coils, or pieces the entire figure is then covered carefully with strips of newspaper which have been dipped into the wallpaper paste. Several complete coatings are essential for a good strong figure. The wallpaper paste adds considerable strength to the figure and gives it a hard surface on which to paint. Some teachers like to put a final coat of torn paper toweling over the whole surface for a better painting surface. While this may be desirable it certainly is not necessary. Finally the figures are allowed to dry for a number of days and are then painted. The teacher should encourage the children to be brave in their selection of colors and not limit them to doing realistic interpretations. When the teacher shows freedom in her approach to problems such as this the feeling is contagious and the children soon learn to work freely and experimentally. During the days through which the figures are drying the teacher should encourage the children to bring from home scrap materials which they think might be useful in adding a final touch of decoration to their papier mache figures. This search for new uses for old materials once again is just another part of the teacher's daily job in developing the sensitivity of each of her children to the things about them.

This individual inventiveness and imaginative thinking is basic to the value of craft teaching.

Some teachers and art educators may be concerned by such specific directions as were illustrated in the preceding example, but the business of learning to follow directions well still has an important place in the classroom. There are many arts and crafts projects which need a balance of directed and creative activities. Any project which remains entirely a directed activity would have very questionable value in the modern classroom. However, if the teacher through good, solid directions can help each child get a good foundation on which to build creatively, then the directed activities are entirely justified in the classroom. It is foolish to think that materials can be placed before children and a command or suggestion made to suffice as a creative motivation. There will be some children in every classroom who could begin to do creative craft work with this minimum sort of motivation, but the teacher who pays attention to individual differences in her classroom is quick to realize there are many youngsters who would have successive failures through this type of laissez faire teaching. There is nothing quite so discouraging as a project which falls apart about halfway through the lesson because of insufficient care or time taken to develop the beginning steps. Some children may have the patience to begin again but most children become discouraged with this sort of experience and are ready to accept the failure and to discontinue the creative experience. Most classroom teachers are aware of the fact that some children become accustomed to habitual failure and lose all confidence in the creative work. The teacher needs to pay a great deal of attention to the differences in children and to see that each child gets sufficient encouragement and direction to help him in his project to the point where he can create successfully, thus providing each child with that feeling of self-confidence that he really desires. The age level at which papier mache can be used depends upon the classroom situation. However, it is seldom possible to do successful papier mache work below the third grade level.

Simple, Bulky Figures

With the smallest children the first experiences in papier mache should be limited to simple, bulky figures such as birds, ducks, rabbits, mice, and the like. Small children might begin by stuffing small paper bags with wads of newspapers to form the main body of the animal or bird and then to make additional small wads of newspaper for the head. This head could be fastened to the first body section by taking long strips of newspaper about an inch wide, dipping them into wallpaper paste, and fastening them across the head wad and down along the body. This process is repeated until sufficient strips have been used to make the head firm and substantial. Children can think about the additional appendages which they might desire and can create them from folded paper if

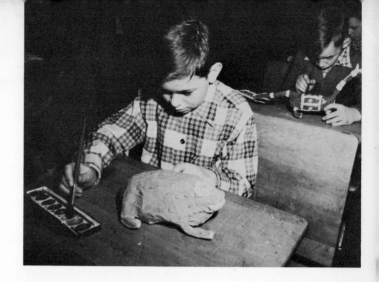

When the teacher encourages a creative climate even a one-room school can have top quality arts and crafts work.

they are to be wings or tails, or from other small wads if they are to be legs or ears or a nose. They can repeat the process using the long strips of newspaper, dipped in paste, to attach each of the additional appendages. Again the more creative children will think of a multitude of uses for the paper and will develop many variations while the slow child may content himself with a simple head and body form which he paints or decorates simply. The slow child may find ample satisfaction in the painting of the face and may gain his creative satisfaction in this way. However, even if this is the case the teacher will consider this a successful creative project if she finds that each child in the class has achieved his limits within the project presented.

Standups

Upper elementary grades and in the junior high school the children enjoy making standup papier maches. To prepare for standup papier maches the teacher should have each child bring two metal coat hangers to class, a piece of scrap wood at least eight inches square and an inch thick, and some newspapers. Most teachers would make this an assignment for several children in order to be

Papier mache stand-ups are easily adapted to action figures and are especially good in the age group in which children are interested in costumes and uniforms.

assured that all the materials would be present on the day of the project. The teacher would need a good pair of wire cutters or lineman's pliers which might be borrowed from the school shop or if not available through this source may ask some child to bring in a pair belonging to a parent. She will need some metal staples of the type used to attach wire fencing to wooden posts. These should be about half an inch in length and can be acquired at any hardware store. The coat hangers should be cut in advance by several of the stronger boys. It is impossible to press a wire cutter completely through a coat hanger wire but only necessary to score it then bend it and it will break at the spot where it has been scored with the wire cutters. These coat hangers are then opened up to their fullest length making each of them about two or two and a nalf feet long. At one end of each wire the boys can bend a small circular shape which will serve as a foot and provide a good means of fastening the foot to the board with the staples. Now as the class begins each child is given his two pieces of wire which he can fasten to the board by means of the staples. Even at this point decisions must be made for this figure may be one which is to stand on one foot, such as a ballet dancer or a running football player, or it may become a football player who is crouching with both feet touching on the ground. When the decision is made the children fasten the wires the distance apart they think the feet should be. Now two coils are made by rolling newspaper, as earlier described in this chapter. These coils would be as long as the coat hangers. They are slipped down over the wires and slid all the way to the feet. They can be temporarily joined about where the waist of the figure will be and the upper parts of the coils can be bent around to form the arms. At this point we have a headless figure but one with two arms and two legs. Now the child should be encouraged to manipulate, to change, to try to achieve action or to develop a pose which is compatible with the type of figure which he intends to make. It may be necessary to loosen one of the feet or to change its position. The flexibility of the project at this time lends itself to a great deal of imaginative thinking. The child may make a small third coil and attach a snowball sized wad to the end of it by means of sticky tape and slip this coil between the shoulders of the first two coils and fasten it into place permanently to form the neck and head. Now the procedure is similar to all other papier mache. Large wads are added where the figure needs to be bulky, details are added and built up, and finally the entire figure is covered with strips of paper dipped in paste. This project invariably adds some additional interesting facets and creates a number of new problems, particularly that of dressing the figures. The teacher will be surprised by the great variety of good and interesting solutions to dressing these figures that the children will come up with, the variety of scrap materials which the children can discover and put to new use.

Such a project can be very successfully correlated with certain social studies units or language units in the elementary school. These will make most unusual center pieces or table decorations for parties or banquets or will provide fine window displays for certain seasonal events.

Papier Mache Miniatures

In many of our schools space, especially storage space, is of great concern where class sizes have exceeded the planned space. In such instances the teacher may wish to use papier mache but keep the projects as small as possible, yet allow for creative experiences in this medium. Many teachers are confused by the idea of bigness and sometimes think bigness and goodness or bigness and creativeness are synonymous. This is not the case, for creativeness is not determined by size. To do small papier mache animals the teacher might provide each child with about a yard length of stove pipe wire. This wire is a soft annealed iron wire available in any hardware store. Its flexibility and ease of bending makes it effective for use by children. The wire is used for an armature or framework within the papier mache. It is best if one builds the entire armature from a single piece of wire. This avoids parts falling off or slipping out

Miniature papier maches are just as effective as large ones and can serve different purposes. Creativeness is not dependent upon size.

of place. The long piece of wire is bent in half and at the bend it is grasped between the thumb and forefinger and twisted for several inches. This portion will serve as the head-neck parts of the papier mache. Twist as little as necessary to form the neck portion of the figure to be built. Now the remainder of the two wires are separated and about five inches along the wire from the last twist one of the pieces is again bent double and twisted in the same fashion that the head-neck portion was twisted. This forms one of the forelegs or arms of the figure. The process is repeated on the other strand of wire so that both legs or arms, as the case may be, are of the same length. Now the two strands are wrapped together again to form what will be the body section, and at this point the child decides whether it is going to be a long body or a short body. After this has been twisted for three or four inches the strands are again separated and going out four or five inches again from the last twist one strand is folded or bent double again and twisted as in the other legs or arms. This will form one of the back legs; using the second strand, the last leg is completed. At this time there will be short strands left on each side which are twisted together to form a tail. Now by bending these sets of legs together the child should have a wire sculpture which can stand firmly. Children will want to manipulate these, create types of animals or figures, some sitting, some standing, some running, until they are satisfied with a position they want to develop. Now papier mache strips can be used directly over the wire and the figure is built up as previously described. These should be neat, compact little papier maches but certainly if presented well should be in every way as creative as any of the other types.

Balloons and Papier Mache

Sometimes, for variety, the teacher may wish to make hollow or "piggy-bank" papier mache animals. By acquiring a variety of shapes of inexpensive balloons, one for each child, the teacher will have the basis for an interesting body shape. The balloons are inflated and very carefully covered with three of four layers of

This balloon papier mache presents a problem in closure. The child has a basic shape to start with and must develop his own ideas about completing that shape.

papier mache to form the main shape and then, as needed, additional body parts are added such as a wad for a head, small wads for legs, coils for long necks or legs. These papier maches are developed as the others described in this chapter and when dry are very, very light but exceedingly strong. Some teachers actually do cut a slot in the back of these so that the children may use these as piggy-banks. This procedure can be used to develop such things as papier mache globes and will be further described under Mask Making.

Giant Size Papier Maches

There are sometimes occasions which demand an unusually large papier mache. This may be the result of group thinking where the children want a large Santa Claus and reindeer, or a Mexican burrow, or perhaps a prehistoric animal. There are absolutely no limitations on the size to which a papier mache can be built as anyone who has ever seen a Mummer's Parade will testify. Normally to do a large sized one in a classroom requires construction of the basic framework or body by means of tables or boxes and the modeling of the basic shape over this with chicken wire or poultry mesh. This wire screening is very easy to work and to manipulate and can be cut with tin snips or wire cutters very easily. Considerable care must be exercised because of the sharp prongs or points which remain after the wire has been cut. It is easy to scratch oneself with these loose, sharp points. However, this should not deter the teacher from using wire screening to accomplish her goal for if the children doing the modeling with the wire wear gloves there is little danger of a scratch on their hands. Once the basic shape has been developed and covered with the chicken wire the entire form can be covered with large pieces of newspaper dipped in paste. This can be worked out through the use of committees or small groups of individuals working during their free time periods. If these large figures are made well enough and coated heavily with shellac or varnish after they are complete and perfectly dry they should be sufficiently water proof to be placed outdoors for short periods of time, a week, perhaps two. For example, a large Santa or snowman which may have decorated the classroom for several weeks prior to Christmas could be shellaced and placed in the school yard during the Christmas holidays. If it deteriorates during this period it is unimportant, for the usefulness of the figure probably has been fulfilled by this time.

Miscellaneous Papier Mache

There are many times during the school year when one of the regular units of work might be enriched or made more meaningful through a special project such as the development of a model, or the making of a relief map, or the building of a diorama. In many instances papier mache may be the very material which most easily solves the problem. The teacher can make a papier mache pulp by soaking bits of torn paper in water and allowing it to stand until the paper has absorbed sufficient water to make it soft and pulpy. The excess water is then drained off and wallpaper paste can be mixed directly into the pulp. This mixture can then be applied to a piece of masonite or plywood and handled a good deal as one would handle clay in modeling mountains or valleys or whatever the problem may call for. It is always better to have heavy boards such as masonite or plywood to work on because the great amount of moisture in the papier mache will wrinkle up a cardboard and destroy its effectiveness. Many times the teacher can solve the problem of providing a small stage prop by constructing a bowl or a goblet or a shield or a helmet by adapting one of the procedures earlier described.

Mask Making

Masks are perhaps one of the most universal of all art forms. Almost every primitive culture uses masks as part of their basic ceremonies. Many of the units which children study in the elementary school concern themselves with cultures and peoples who have used masks as part of their daily rituals and in their special ceremonies. Masks play a significant part of the African cultures and the Eskimo and Indian cultures. Masks are used widely in dramatics and in the theatre in the culture of the Greeks and Japanese and in India. The teacher should capitalize on the universality of masks to make a classroom project to provide a means of personal self-expression for each of the children and to develop a better understanding of other cultures and other peoples through the use of masks. Any craft project which is done simply for the sake of doing it or only to acquire skills may be of questionable value. In no case should the teacher ever allow the product to become an end in itself, for creative work in crafts as in art, requires also a meaningful process to have educational value. Each project should be thought through sufficiently to provide for as many of the basic objectives of art education and education as possible. Every good teacher knows that we begin with children as we find them and seek to broaden their horizons only as rapidly as they are able to assimilate meaningful experiences. Therefore, when we would start mask making with our smallest children we would do so with reference only to those things which might have meaning to the children. The smallest children would understand masks most through their experiences in Halloween parades and parties and this would be the logical point of departure in mask making. Later as their interests and understandings broaden the teacher would refer to mask making in American culture of American Indians, Canadian Indians, finally Alaskan and Canadian Eskimos and as the world still grows smaller for the children the cultures of other countries would be brought in pointing out the significance of these masks in the various cultures.

The simplest materials often give the greatest satisfaction. The child who learns to use a variety of materials in school is most often found doing creative work at home.

Paper Bags Again

The easiest way to start in making masks is with the ordinary paper bag if the teacher can acquire a sufficient number of large paper bags so that each child might have one large enough to slip over his head. If these are very large bags it might be desirable to cut an inverted U shape from each of the two sides so that it can slip down over the shoulders of the child. By touching with his fingers the child can locate the position of his eyes and with a crayon gently mark for eye openings on the bag. Now we get into the project of cutting and pasting paper, developing eyes, nose, mouth, hair, and ears as completely as each child is capable. There is no need here to encourage the children to deviate from reality for with the small children this is a normal procedure. Green noses and purple lips are commonplace and should be accepted. The teacher should always be careful not to impose her own tastes or standards upon the children, who are discovering these things for themselves. Paper bag masks can be just as easily painted or decorated with crayons if cut paper and paste has been much used before, or is unavailable. Sometimes a bit of raffia, shavings from the wood shop, strands of yarn, or a bit of ribbon can be used to really set off the finished mask. The teacher keeps a box of these interesting materials in her classroom. Even the smallest children will quickly find interesting uses for them in their constructions. A milk bottle cap will soon become a nose or a scrap of colored cellophane a hair ribbon. This type of mask is easily accomplished in one period and always proves to be very exciting and interesting for the children.

Try a Paper Plate

The very shape of a paper plate or picnic plate and the fact that almost every household has a half dozen left over from last summer's picnics make the paper plate mask a good one to try in the middle elementary grades. To give these some three-dimensional quality, two slits about two inches deep are cut in the edge of the plate. These slits should be about two or three inches apart. If the sides adjacent to each slit are overlapped slightly and stapled back together again this forms a simple chin cup or shape which makes the mask fit nicely on the child's face. The child can locate and mark the position of his eyes by means of touch. Later, with the point of the scissors make incisions for the eyes. The teacher might illustrate methods by which the nose can be cut on the bottom and two sides and flapped out for an interesting three-dimensional quality, or how a hole might be cut in the center where the nose normally would be and other types of noses, such as a cone, pyramid, or box, or simply a crumpled wad, developed from construction paper. These first experiments in three-dimensional paper work or paper sculpture will lead to interesting improvisions for eyebrows, for hair, for cheeks, and for ears. The teacher should encourage the children at this point to experiment three-dimensionally with the paper in as many ways as possible and to develop these masks as a project in paper sculpture. The edges of the paper can be embellished by feathers or fur or cotton or hair to get interesting effects for the particular type of mask the child is making. Again a scrap box with such things as raffia and yarns, shavings, steel wool, will be invaluable in suggesting new and different approaches to mask making. If these materials are not available paint and crayons could suffice to make very interesting and very exciting masks. Whenever possible, the teacher ought to encourage children to deviate from reality using the masks of other cultures as illustrations of her point, asking the children to create a mood or a feeling suggest that they make it look mean or make it look happy or make it look sad rather than make it look "real." Finally, a rubber band can be stapled to each side and joined with a piece of string to hold the mask in place, or two pieces of string can be stapled to each side and tied around the child's head to hold the mask in place.

More Balloons

A balloon which can be inflated larger than a child's head makes a wonderful base for large and interesting masks. If the child can bring a balloon of this type, it is inflated until it is somewhat larger than the child's head. The balloon is then covered with three or four carefully applied layers of papier mache and put aside to dry. This foundation is made first. It is much easier for the children to go on working on the hard layer at a later time. When it is dry and hard and strong the children can then begin to develop the type of mask they want to make. The round shape could easily become a lion or a bear or a person or a pumpkin. Using the standard methods of papier mache making earlier described, the children can develop whatever creature they wish from this basic shape. After this has dried sufficiently and has hardened the teacher, using a razor blade or X-acto knife, must cut a hole in the bottom of the mask large enough for the child to slip his head through. The balloon may then be removed. When the

A large balloon makes a mask into which the child can slip his whole head with ease.

mask fits, openings made for visibility can be easily disguised in the painting of the mask. This kind of mask would probably be best decorated with a good quality of poster paint or tempera paint, and finally decorated with bits of scrap materials as we have seen before.

This same procedure can be used to make globes.

Gummed Paper Masks

One of the most effective and best fitting masks can be done in the upper elementary grades. This project requires the use of a quantity of gummed kraft tape, tissue paper or cloth, and papier mache. This project is generally begun with a demonstration by the teacher with one of the pupils as the subject. A large piece of cloth or tissue wrapping paper sufficient to cover the face and hair is placed on one of the children. A variety of lengths from two feet down to about six inches of gummed tape are ready for the demonstration, and a piece of paper towelling which has been soaked in water is ready for moistening the gummed tape. The teacher begins by placing the piece of cloth or paper over the child's face and hair. Then, with a two foot long piece of gummed tape which she has moistened, she carefully goes around from under the chin up over the top of the head forming an oval shape. This is pressed down firmly and repeated several times. Now shorter strips are run from one side of the face to the other side of the face joining the oval from side to side. Now some of the strips are run from top to bottom. By now a definite half spherical shape has been developed, one which actually has the form of the head. At this point it can be removed from the child's head and wadded newspaper placed inside it to give

Teamwork is the starting point for gummed tape and papier mache masks. These "tailor-made" masks always fit well and have limitless variations.

added strength while working on it and the teacher can demonstrate how, through the use of sticky paper, much of the basic shape can be then developed before starting with the papier mache. For example, short strips can be buckled and very carefully built up to any size or shape to form a nose. The same procedure can be used to demonstrate eyebrows, eyes, mouth, or chin. Finally, when the basic shape has been developed, the child can go to work using papier mache strips and pieces. Now the children pair off and repeat this process on each other until each has his own fitted mask to develop. The teacher should be careful to lay a good ground work for the understanding of the meaning of masks and may have illustrations on the bulletin board of primitive masks, or may have shown a film such as "The Loon's Necklace."* All this background will help break down certain stereotypes which might prevail otherwise. Excess cloth is finally removed, the excess tissue paper is cut away and the masks can then

* *The Loon's Necklace.* 11 min., color, published by Encyclopaedia Brittanica Films. How the blind old medicine man gives his magic necklace to the loon is told by a narrator and enacted by silent actors, wearing primitive British Columbian Indian masks. (May be rented from almost any educational film library.)

be painted and decorated as in other projects. This particular type of mask can be used very effectively in small dramas which the children can develop themselves. The masks can even be mounted on long sticks which are painted black and very exciting plays can be worked out against a black background using a darkened room and a flood light to light up the stage area. The children can keep out of sight kneeling behind a table and can manipulate their mask heads against the black background for a most exciting performance.

These procedures which have been illustrated are only a few of the many possibilities in mask making. These are, however, good tried basic ones and can be a stepping-off point for many other varieties which the teacher may wish to try on other occasions.

WEAVING, HOOKING,

STITCHERY,

AND APPLIQUE

8

THE HISTORY of weaving is as old as history itself. Social studies would hardly be complete without including some study of weaving. There is no better way for children to understand and to appreciate the art and craftsmanship of weaving than by actually creating with yarns and fibres. The main object of teaching weaving in the elementary school should never be the creation of a finished project, but rather the gaining of experience through exploration of a new medium. Even with the youngest children the approach to weaving should be exploratory. It is the responsibility of the teacher to seek and provide the most suitable materials for the age level which will use them—large, simple materials for use with the younger children, and a greater variety of textures and types of yarns for the older ones. Even at the very beginning as the child handles the materials and begins to sense the qualities of yarn and to understand its possibilities, he begins making important decisions. He chooses colors, combining and arranging them in his own best way. Here the teacher should constantly seek to stimulate the imagination and thinking by asking simple questions such as "Which colors do you think would be best for you?" or "Can you arrange them in an interesting way?" Some teachers limit the weaving experiences of children to simple paper mats, but many children find paper weaving rather difficult to do because of the flimsiness of the paper, and others may not derive a sufficient satisfaction from the finished product.

A Simple Wooden Loom

To construct a good simple loom you need only four pieces of wood, some finishing nails, some string, and, of course, you will need rug yarn for weaving. Begin with two strips of wood about ¾″ × 1½″ × 12″ long, and two pieces 16″ to 18″ long. Nail the two short pieces to the two longer pieces so as to form a rectangular frame. Drive several nails into each corner of the frame to make it strong. Down the center of the top surface of the short strips mark a dot with a pencil every half inch. Following this, drive inch long finishing nails at the dots half way into the wood and slant them toward the outside of the loom. The loom is now ready to be strung, or "warped."

Start at any corner and tie your string to the corner nail. Stretch it to the opposite side and go around the backs of *two* nails, bring it back again and loop it behind nails number two and number three, then back to the opposite side and so on until you have completed stringing the loom. This will put the warp threads parallel at half inch intervals, making it reasonably easy for the children to use well. Use cotton roving or cotton rug yarn of a heavy type about one

Weaving helps develop sensitivity to materials, color, and design while helping to develop manual dexterity.

quarter inch in diameter and cut it into lengths about 4″ longer than the outside strings on the loom. If these are precut and piled freely in the box the child can select the colors which are most agreeable to him and can begin to weave on one end. It takes only minutes to explain the process of weaving so the children understand it. When the weaving is complete, packed firm and tight, it can be removed from the loom. At this time the teacher should stitch each end with the sewing machine, if possible, or have one of the mothers do it. The ends can be trimmed neatly with shears and the child is the proud possessor of a fine table mat. The same principles just described could be used on a piece of cardboard, where notches cut in each end to hold the string are used instead of nails. Since this would be a smaller type loom the notches would be placed about a quarter of an inch apart and finer yarn and a needle could be used for the weaving process. When using this type of loom, if a tongue depressor or ice cream stick is slipped under all of the warp at each end, this will lift the warp from the cardboard and make it a great deal easier for the child to weave.

Soda Straws or Macaroni

A fine bookmark or even a belt can be made using soda straws or long hollow macaroni as the loom. Give each child about six soda straws or pieces of long hollow macaroni and give each a piece of heavy wool or cotton yarn about two feet long for each soda straw. The yarn is threaded through each soda straw by tying a bit of thread to the center of each piece of yarn and pulling the yarn through the soda straws so that each straw has a loop appearing out of one end and two loose ends appearing out of the other. Now, take the twelve loose ends

The principles of weaving are soon understood by the child who works on the most basic project. Retarded children can learn to weave well.

and tie them together as a tassel. Then using another piece of yarn for weaving, the six straws are held together and a process of going over-under-over-under is begun. When the sixth straw is reached the yarn is simply looped over and worked back; when the first straw is again reached the yarn is looped over and worked back again. When the weaving is long enough the straws are slipped out one by one and the looped ends of the yarn are tied together in another tassel. To make a belt in this manner, it is necessary to use much longer lengths of yarn but the process is essentially the same. However, when the soda straws are about three quarters covered with weaving they are slipped along leaving only about a quarter of their length still covered by the weaving. This, then, permits the student to go on covering another portion before moving the straws on again. This process is repeated until the entire length of the yarns have been woven.

A Cardboard Purse Loom

In the upper elementary grades children can use the cardboard purse loom very effectively to make handsome and practical purses or bags. These can be made in any size or shape but, for purposes of explanation, a purse which is 5″ × 8″ finished will be described. Each child is given a piece of cardboard 6″ × 8″. Holding this piece horizontally on the desk, from the top edge of the piece measure down one half inch from each of the two top corners and mark. Join these marks with a line. Do exactly the same thing from the bottom, measuring from the bottom up. You now have a cardboard with two horizontal lines running across it, one a half inch from the top and the other a half inch from the bottom. Along each of these lines place a ruler and carefully mark each quarter inch until the end of the cardboard is reached. Using the ruler, draw lines on top and

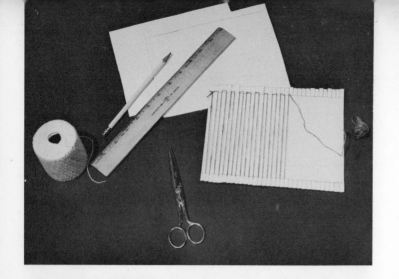

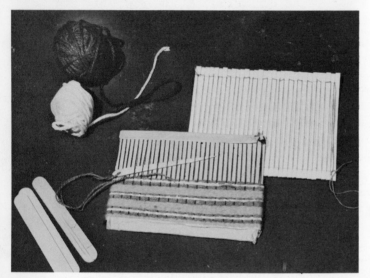

bottom reaching from the half-inch mark to the edge of the cardboard on each quarter-inch marking. The scissors are used to cut these down exactly to the half inch mark. The cardboard now should appear with rows of notches, top and bottom, a half inch deep. Now to string the loom. If the teacher has available ordinary cotton warp this is excellent; however, kite string or string about that weight is excellent for this purpose. The color is immaterial. Tie one end of this string to the first tab in the upper left hand corner of the cardboard using a simple loop and knot to attach it. Now, bring the warp down the front of the cardboard and through the first notch at the bottom. This puts the string to the back of the loom. Come up the back and go into the first notch at the top. This makes a complete trip around the loom returning to the spot where it started. Now the warp is hanging on the front of the loom. Loop it into notch number two at the top and now it is hanging down the back of the loom. Take it through notch number two at the bottom and up the front to notch number two at the top. Go through notch number two at the top and now the yarn is in the back of the loom. Loop it into notch number three at the top and now it is hanging down the front of the loom. Bring it down the front into notch number three at the bottom, go through notch number three taking it to the back, and return again to notch number three at the top bringing it through to the front. Loop it again into notch number four down the back and into notch number four at the bottom, up the front and into notch number four at the top. By this time the sequence should become clear. The warped strings run parallel front and back, loops appear at the top at alternate spaces both front and back.

When the loom is completely strung across to the last notch, front and back, the remaining string will be at the top of the loom. Now it is necessary to create one additional thread so that the weaving can progress properly. Therefore, go down once more to the bottom corner and tie the string to the last tab at the bottom, the same as the one at the beginning. This makes one notch with a double thread on one side only. Later, when weaving, these two threads or warps will be used as two separate warps in the same way that any other two warps on the loom would be used separately.

To insure the tabs from not being broken off during the handling of the weaving process it is a good idea to use gummed tape, scotch tape, or masking tape and go down both rows of tabs front and back with a strip. Now to weave! A good weaving needle can be made from an ice cream stick or half a tongue depressor, split lengthwise, which has been sharpened and sandpapered and into which a small hole has been drilled for the insertion of the yarn. It is important to make a good weaving needle because it simplifies the work and makes it progress much more rapidly. With a threaded needle that has about a yard of yarn in it, begin someplace near the middle of the loom at the bottom. Run under about three or four threads and then begin the process of going over-under-over-under-over-under. When the last thread is reached check what was done on the last thread, whether it was over or under. Turn the loom over and continue around the end keeping the same sequence of over-under-over-under used on the front. When, finally, the double thread is reached it must be treated as two separate threads. Go over one, under the second and continue the sequence around and around until the thread has reached its end. Tuck the remaining bit of thread under the warps, rethread the needle, run under three or four lines, and begin again. It is not necessary and even undesirable to tie the different pieces of yarn together. The loose ends will be hidden inside and will never pull out. Design is limited in this type of loom and almost always consists of horizontal lines and changes of color or texture. However, after one or two projects some children will devise techniques which are astounding to make designs in this type of purse loom. When the weaving has reached the top the teacher should see that it has been packed down carefully as it goes along, using a comb or the fingernails or a fork. Pack it so tightly that none of the warp appears through it. The last few rows will have to be done with a steel darning needle, so that they can be filled as completely as possible. When no more weaving can be done the tabs are torn off top and bottom. At the top the loops will open up and the cardboard can be slipped out. The purse will be complete, both sides will be finished and the bottom will be finished. For the smaller children, tape with snaps may be sewed in to complete the purse, or they may wish to have help at home in lining it. With the older children the lining is more important and perhaps a zipper can be sewn into the purse for a fine finish. This project becomes so popular that once begun some of the children will finish three or four purses. Each time they will seek to do a better job than on the one before, and the quality of this product is invariably very high.

Some teachers question the advisability of sending a project home with the child for additional help by a parent. There are times when such an approach is a very desirable one. There is no better way for a parent to gain insight into the importance of the child's way of thinking and the value of art for children than through participating jointly in a project which is very important and meaningful to the child. It is only through this close relationship that the parent can fully appreciate the meaning of art in child education.

On an Oatmeal or Salt Box

The teacher who has mastered the procedure of the purse loom can make a splendid modification by using an oatmeal box in place of the flat cardboard. Here the markings are made around the top and bottom of the box in the same way as for the flat purse. It is strung by tying an end of string to one of the notches at the top, going down to the bottom, across the bottom, and directly up the other side, into a notch, looped over into the next notch, down the side, and across the bottom, and up the other side. A few minutes of experimenting with this will easily show the teacher the answer to stringing this loom. Actually,

A container of almost any shape can be strung as a loom and covered with weaving.

this is considerably easier than the earlier loom for there is no turning over of the loom when reaching the end. The child simply weaves around and around until he reaches the top where the tabs are torn off, the loops loosened, and the cardboard box removed or partially removed, trimmed, and reinserted to help the weaving keep its shape. This type of loom offers a large variety of possibilities for weaving or yarn boxes. Excellent draw string purses can be made, and interesting modifications can be made by making short ones and sewing a tube of corduroy or velveteen to the top of them for handsome draw string purses.

Hooking

Rug hooking offers the teacher another opportunity to allow the children to design for "something" rather than the designing for "nothing" which has occupied so much of the art time in the classrooms of American schools for so many years. Rug hooking generally begins with the design conceived with chalk or thick tempera or torn colored paper. Teachers should encourage the same freedom in developing designs as she would in encouraging free painting or drawing. When the child creates a design which is not too tedious or too detailed to be worked out he can nail together a hooking frame from strips of wood, or he may use an old picture frame or sturdy embroidery hoops as the frames. A piece of burlap bag is stretched across the frame and stapled or tacked firmly to it and the sketch for the design applied with a crayon. Hooking can be done with yarns or thrums, strips of stocking which have been dyed, strips of rags, or strips of wool jersey. The hooking is done with a crochet or hooking tool. These are available in any dry goods or ten cent store.

The process of hooking is very simple. The yarn or strips of rag are held beneath the burlap in one hand, the crochet hook or hooking tool is inserted through the burlap, caught into the strip and pulled up into a loop on the top. The needle goes through the burlap the second time hooking the strand again and pulling it up. After a dozen or so strokes the person hooking learns to judge the proper distance along the strand at which to attach the hook so that each loop is uniform in height. The hooking is done in sufficient closeness to pack the loops in so they will not pull out. The different types of rags and wools will produce different types of textured areas of color and of pile, and as this occurs the children will modify their designs. The project remains creative to the end and is not merely a mechanical process. As the child hooks he will create problems for himself, but he will also discover solutions for himself.

When the small mat is finished the back can be coated with a rubberized liquid to hold all the loops in place, but this is not necessary. The remaining burlap edges can be turned under and sewed into place. Although children are encouraged in the beginning to work on small mats they usually will want to go on to a larger rug. Rug hooking can be a fascinating and absorbing experience if it is approached creatively in design and construction. It can be a tedious master if it is a purely mechanical process based on commercially prepared designs.

Stitchery and Embroidery

Webster defines *embroider* "as to ornament with needlework, also to form by needlework or to embellish or ornament." Embroidery is an old craft used by the ancient Egyptians and is even described in the Old Testament. Its earliest uses were primarily to decorate wearing apparel. As a craft it has flourished primarily

This stitchery which shows children skating on a pond is reminiscent of the needle work of European children of the 1930's.

112

A drab piece of burlap is turned into a fabric of charm by the addition of some yarn, rick-rack, netting and sequins, and the imagination of childhood. (Courtesy Arts and Activities and Hilda G. Rosenberg, Chicago, Ill.)

in peasant cultures and is most often thought of as a peasant art, and in this country in the past half dozen decades embroidery was generally relegated to the housewife as a pastime and seldom was it recognized as a real art form. In recent years, however, needlework and embroidery have suddenly been revitalized and many people are using it as a pure art form. Beautiful examples are to be found particularly in churches. The stitchery which was done when grandmother was a child generally consisted of stitching old fashioned samplers, fancy doilies, and prepared tapestry designs. The entire emphasis was placed upon making neat and accurate stitches and carefully following the prepared color arrangements and stamped patterns. This sort of meticulous busy work would give little satisfaction or be of value to the children of today, who need to be challenged and who need to be presented with problems so that they may seek their own solutions. Todays approach to stitchery should be exploratory in nature. The teacher should try to acquire and provide the materials best suited to the age of her children, and to provide an atmosphere suitable for creative work. To learn to copy and to imitate is one thing but to be original and to follow one's own envisioned plan, to keep ones own ideas flowing, to think, to decide, to change, to be filled with the excitement of unknown possibilities ahead, to develop a plan and a design, and then to execute it, this is creativity at work. With the young child working on loosely woven materials such as burlap or monk's cloth, and with large tapestry needles and yarns of many colors, the teacher may begin by motivating the children's imagination and thinking by asking some simple questions. "What can you do with these yarns?" "What can you do to make your materials gay and beautiful?" "Who can think of a stitch to make?" Through these initial experiments the child can discover that his needle can go in and out, under and over, over three and under one, under three and over one. Soon his ingenuity and resourcefulness will help

Almost any craft can be adapted to group thinking and working. (Courtesy Arts and Activities and Lillie B. Adams, Atlanta, Ga.)

him invent stitches and to combine and select colors which are as personal as the lines and colors that he makes in his child paintings. In his stitchery the child will most likely develop in his ability to work in the same way that he developed in his drawing and painting activities, beginning first with simple lines, later creating areas or shapes, finally creating textures and surfaces. He may begin in a rather disorganized fashion and work towards an organized design in the same way that his first paintings may have been disorganized and later became organized. As his designs develop on the material he may find it necessary to occasionally bring in an accent like a small bit of felt or a bead or an artificial pearl to develop his ideas to the fullest. As in other crafts, the slow child may limit his thinking to simple running lines while the more creative child will quickly get the feel of the material and develop beautiful color relationships, textures, and a variety of stitches. As stitchery develops from the lower grades to the upper grades the variety of projects widens. While the first projects may be purely decorative or pictorial wall hangings, later on material can be used for crayon bags, purses, knitting bags, and even large projects with a group such as curtains or drapes. The opportunities with stitchery are limitless and one needs only to try it once to discover the many possibilities that it holds.

Applique

Applique is a process in which pieces of one fabric are applied or laid on, sewed, or pasted onto another. The fact that small children love to sew and that most homes have large quantities of scrap rags of various colors and sizes which can be acquired simply for the asking, makes applique an interesting and useful craft project for the elementary school. Since applique deals primarily with shapes and flat areas rather than the linear quality of the stitch, designs can be worked out with colored paper in advance of the actual cutting and sewing. Once the design has been decided upon, pieces of material to match the colored paper can be selected and cut to size, pinned on to the basic cloth or burlap, and sewn in place. It is always wise for the teacher to encourage the children to make changes as they go along, keeping the project spontaneous to the very end and not merely a mechanical process. Changing from paper to cloth may suggest new ideas and the use of a particular stitch on the edge may suggest another possibility. Even the addition of stitches over portions of the cloth may create new textures and solve problems which arise. Applique can be used for wall hangings or drapes, for aprons and purses. If the teacher is near a large city she can probably acquire great quantities of wonderful scrap cloth by visiting dress factories and may acquire excellent felt scraps by visiting hat manufacturers. Sometimes this material is simply thrown away or burned and it can be had for the asking. When the teacher is able to acquire a quantity of felt hat scraps she

Stitchery combined with applique makes a wall hanging. (Courtesy Arts and Activities and Hilda G. Rosenberg, Chicago, Ill.)

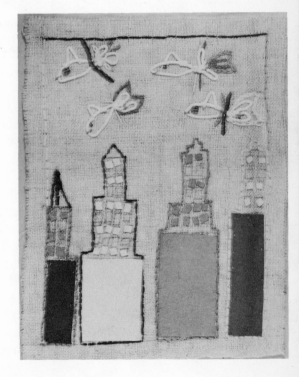

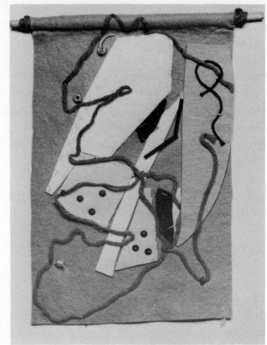

Applique wall hangings show some of the combinations which are possible with a few materials. (Courtesy Arts and Activities and Pat T. Cravey, Atlanta, Ga.)

may find many useful applications in the making of mittens, slippers, head bands, comb cases, glasses cases, and purses. The felt can be used as applique on each of the stitchery projects mentioned before. Lack of classroom materials should not be considered a handicap but rather thought of as a challenge, for the teacher who explores her neighborhood will find endless quantities of use- able materials which can be had simply by asking. Good art programs are always built on ingenuity, resourcefulness, initiative, and imaginative use of waste materials. One can seldom attribute a poor art or craft program to a lack of anything other than the teacher's own resourcefulness.

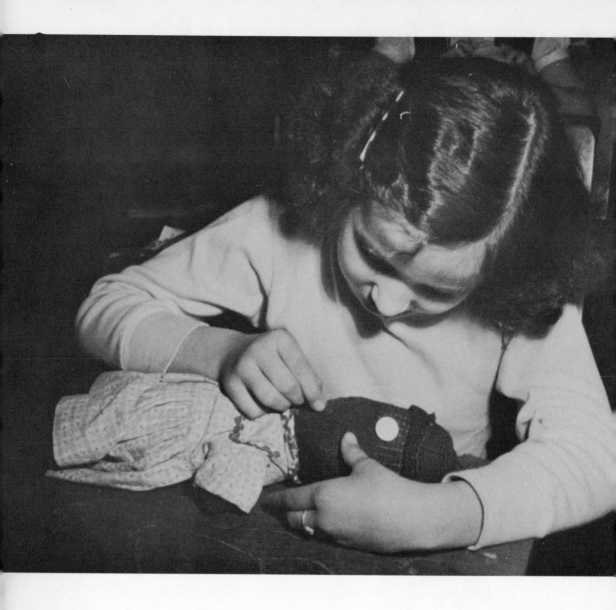

POTPOURRI

9

THIS CHAPTER discusses several additional projects and methods that will enrich and make more varied any crafts program. They are grouped here in one chapter because the individual treatments are not sufficiently lengthy to warrant separate chapters. Here, as elsewhere, the teacher can help the children develop their own techniques.

Collage

The collage is a type of abstraction made with fragments of many types of materials pasted or fastened together into an artistic composition of contrasting textures. The idea of using such materials in a serious fashion first appeared during the First World War when artists and teachers found themselves compelled to experiment with substitute materials because of the absence of good art supplies. This sort of forced improvisation led to a new and interesting phase of experimental art. Many fine and interesting examples of this type of art remain and are exhibited in our major galleries. Perhaps the most recent work of Matisse shows the great effect of the collage upon contemporary art. Teachers know that inexpensive and so-called waste materials and odds and ends like buttons, costume jewelry, ribbons, sequins, rickrack, fabric scraps, and so on, are invaluable in the average classroom. Such materials are best arranged in separate boxes so that like types of materials are grouped together. The child quickly learns to distinguish their special features and uses. Through the use of a variety of materials the child is also able to develop a tactile sense which helps him to distinguish texture and feeling for the different kinds of materials. All the first projects in collage generally result from simple spontaneous motivations excited by the materials, and may often turn into representational projects. The later collage experiments with older children can be guided and many of the principles of design can be incorporated indirectly and emphasized as the need arises. The collage problems in mood or problems in opposites are good ones to work in. Urge the children to express the feeling of excitement or sorrow or cheer through a sensitive selection of colors, sizes, shapes, and by their placement and arrangement on the cardboard background. The problem of opposites will help sensitize the children to the different kinds of materials. A problem which urges them to place large against small, light against dark, or shiny against dull, or rough against smooth, or thick against thin will bring about a greater awareness. Collage projects are often carried to extremes where teachers over-use it or when it becomes an end in itself and especially in those instances where all art becomes nonobjective "designs." Such projects sometimes become very popular because of the rapid and spectacular results from a minimum motivation. The teacher must always be aware that the good program needs balance at all times and while adventures in materials have the utmost importance they can only supplement the good drawing and painting program based upon the individual experiences of the children.

Build with Boxes

At the back of every store, in the basement of every school, in the garage of every home are empty cardboard boxes waiting for small children with big ideas to turn them into houses, or trains, or automobiles, or buses. If the classroom has a corner which needs a special project the class needs only to gather together a half dozen or so cardboard cartons of various sizes to start a box project. "What will it be?" the teacher might ask. "Let's make a house," says John. "Let's make a bunch of trucks," says Billy, and Ann says, "Let's make the schoolhouse."

Boxes are perfect for building "my house" or "our town." A variety of shapes will suggest different kinds of buildings and different treatments.

So we must decide, and when the discussion ends we have decided we will make a train, and the largest box becomes the engine, and another the tender, and there is a freight car, and a passenger car, and a caboose. The teacher says, "Who will make the engine?" "I will," say five, and they do. "Who will make the caboose?" "I will,'" say six, and they do. Using tempera paints and large brushes the children quickly and easily plan and paint their train and soon it is all assembled, tied together with pieces of roving or rope. Tomorrow, during library period, some of the children can sit in the train to read their books. This project is always spontaneous and easy and it takes little motivation on the part of the teacher to make it highly successful.

If the community is served by dairies which use the waxed cardboard quart containers either for store sales or home sales these can be accumulated and

Empty containers can be anything to a child whose imagination is free. To most adults an empty box is an empty box but to the child it is a house, a car, a train, a wagon, an anything. (Courtesy Arts and Activities and Mary Adeline McKibbin, Pittsburgh, Pa.)

Small boxes or milk containers present a different set of problems and can yield good products. (Courtesy School Arts and Dr. John Lembach, College Park, Md.)

used in a variety of ways. By cutting them in different ways the children can make trains and cars and buses and wagons and tables and chairs and cupboards and chests, and may even turn some of them into heads or people. Brass paper fasteners and a stapler are very handy to have in this kind of construction.

121

Art teaches economy of statement and also economy of materials. These paper mosaics simply and beautifully convey the characters of Christmas, yet use only collected scraps of colored paper. (Courtesy School Arts and Pauli Tolman, Los Angeles, Calif.)

Mosaics

Mosaics are surface decorations made of small pieces of colored glass, stone, or other materials inlaid on a surface. The simplest mosaics which could be made in the elementary school would be ones made of small bits of torn or cut colored paper. If the colored paper scrap box seems to be getting overly full the teacher may, on one day, set some of the children cutting it into small pieces on the paper cutter so that the pieces are one half inch square or smaller and making an effort to keep colors separate, if possible, in different small boxes such as cigar boxes, and when a sizable quantity of pieces have been cut the teacher may try a picture in the mosaic method. It would be good to bring in illustrations of mosaics done in the early Byzantine churches or even some contemporary illustrations of mosaics so that the children would understand fully the meaning of the project presented. Also every lesson in crafts should be an opportunity for a lesson in appreciation. Having made a decision about what they will do, the children can begin the project and can select the colors which most nearly satisfy the ideas that they have in mind, starting with the central figure or object, working toward the edges of the upper paper. The mosaics can be more exciting if they are pasted on a background of colored paper or of colored cardboard. Most interesting variations can be made by using sample books of wallpaper cut up in this fashion. The wallpaper books are another excellent source of colored papers which can be had generally for the asking. As the styles and patterns change frequently these are discarded by the wallpaper stores. Slightly more complex mosaics can be made with a variety of materials. If the school is located in a community where interesting gravel and pebbles are to be found or varieties of seeds and pods or types of grain, interesting mosaics can be made by assembling this combination of materials. When the mosaics begin to have weight as do those made of seeds, pebbles or gravel, then it is necessary to change to a type of glue which has greater strength than the ordinary library paste used for paper work. There are quite a number of excellent white liquid glues on the market today under a variety of names. They have a milky appearance. They are easy to use and exceedingly strong.

To make a mosaic using tiles is slightly more complex but not too difficult to try in the upper elementary grades. If a kiln is available in the school children can easily make their own tiles by rolling out clay with a rolling pin, coating it with a one-fire glaze or with an engobe (a colored clay). When it is stiff enough cut it into small rectangles one half inch square or smaller. These can be fired and are thereafter ready for applying to a board. If no kiln is available for firing clay large quantities of scrap tile can be obtained from tile setters. At the end of every day tile setters throw away a large box of scrap tile, the pieces which remain from corners and edges which they have had to cut. Several days' collection of these would provide an adequate supply to begin a ceramic tile mosaic. These can be broken up with a hammer but are best cracked by use of a pair of tile nippers available at any hardware store. The trick of cutting tiles with nippers is to catch only the very edge of the tile in the nippers and snap it rather than grabbing a large portion of tile between the jaws of the nippers. A boy can quickly master the method of cutting tiles. When a sufficient number of small pieces are broken and a design planned and marked off on a piece of plywood or masonite the tile setting begins. It is necessary to build a small wooden wall all around the edge of the plywood to hold the cement in place which goes between the pieces of tile at the very end. Now the tiles are simply glued to the plywood by means of the same white liquid glue that most people have in their households. When the design is complete and firmly set a thin mixture of cement and sand and water, called grout, is poured over the entire mosaic filling all the spaces between the tiles. After it has been worked down into the spaces between

Bathroom tiles are cracked with nippers and fastened in place with waterproof glue onto a plywood.

A bathroom-tile mosaic made by a class of teen-agers after helping produce A Connecticut Yankee in King Arthur's Court as a school play.

the tiles, dry concrete is dusted over the top of this surface and rubbed with a cloth over the entire mosaic. This dry concrete aids in rapid setting of the grout between the tiles and it also cleans the surface of the mosaic at the same time. When this process is complete damp cloths or wet paper towels are placed over the top and allowed to remain for 24 to 48 hours. This prevents cracks from forming in the grout area. Now the mosaic can be scrubbed clean with a scrubbing brush and soap and it is a completed project. Mosaics have become extremely popular in the past few years and many mosaic supplies are available from any school supply house.

Toy Making

In recent years many of the elementary classrooms have been provided with a small work bench or work table, a vise, and a small variety of hand tools such

Making one's own toys has a special appeal to most children. Whether they are of wood or cardboard is of little importance to the child. (Courtesy Baltimore Public Schools and Dr. Leon L. Winslow.)

as a saw, hammer, and pliers. Just a hammer and some nails can be sufficient for making very pleasant little wooden toys. To stimulate the imagination in the making of these toys there should be a scrap box for wooden pieces in the classroom and a periodic visit to the school woodshop or local lumber yard to gather scrap wood. The teacher should try to select interesting shapes of soft wood. Pieces of oak or hickory are impossible for the children to nail and can be extremely frustrating to both teacher and child. It takes little starting to have children begin to build toys or airplanes or boats and the variety of shapes which are in the box will suggest the kind of uses the pieces may be put to. Several cans of bright enamel for the older children can be used for painting. For the younger ones painting is generally limited to water based paints so that if an accident should occur the paint can easily be washed up. When the children make toys to pull along the floor bottle caps can be nailed to the bottom board to serve as gliders or coasters to make it pull along more easily. The youngsters can get as much pleasure out of these homemade toys or even more pleasure than out of their metal or commercial plastic ones. Again the scrap box which contains the buttons and braid and fringe and rickrack and felt scraps and feathers and beads and old costume jewelry will provide very rich and interesting trim and decoration to finish off their wooden toys.

Wind Harps

For many years and even back as far as most of us can remember we have heard oriental wind harps tinkling on Victorian front porches and even today we can find these very nice glass wind harps in the five and ten cent stores or in the city China Towns. Children can make wind harps which sound just as gay and cheerful as the oriental ones. The glass scrap barrel which was mentioned earlier in the chapter on "Holidays and Seasonal Activities" can once again provide material for a creative project. In such a barrel will be many long and slender pieces of clear window glass which can be glamorized with a bit of color here and there, perhaps a thin enamel or one of the commercial paints recommended for use on glass by leading art supply companies. It is not good to

A wind harp involves careful selection of sizes, shapes, colors, and sounds of pieces of glass which are hung in interesting groups so that the pieces touch as they turn.

cover a whole surface for this deadens the tone of the glass. Just a touch of color here and there will do the job best. An even better kind of glass to use can be purchased at a photography shop. It is called cover glass and is used for mounting transparent slides. It comes in pieces about two inches square. This is very light in weight and is tempered. These pieces create a beautiful tinkly tone. A third good source is the scrap from colored glass factories. This can be purchased for a reasonable price and is exceedingly beautiful; however, to use this type of glass the teacher must become proficient in the use of a glass cutter. The pieces of glass can be hung from silk or nylon threads by means of little tabs of brown gummed tape. Generally this tape is sufficiently strong to hold a pretty sizable piece of glass, however, if any doubt exists a small amount of transparent cement may be touched around the edge of the brown tab for added insurance. These pieces of glass must be hung in a cluster so that as the wind moves them they swing sufficiently to touch one another gently and cause a tinkling sound. This project then becomes one of inventing a hanging device which is attractive and which functions. Pieces of heavy wire screening like a lathing screen or a twisted coat hanger or a coffee can lid with many holes punched through it or concentric embroidery hoops or blocks of wood with nails driven into it might be beginning ideas for the development of the hanger. When a good hanger has been developed the threads can be attached to it and the pieces arranged in the most aesthetic manner.

Now two problems come into play, appearance and sound. Sometimes the children need to make visual arrangements, other times they make arrangements based on the sounds of the glass. When completed, these can be hung in a corner of a room near a window and the slightest breeze will create a lovely tinkling sound. When finally taken home they can be hung under a porch roof where they are protected from hard breezes and rain and where slight motions of air make them tinkle all day long. This is also an excellent project in the junior and senior high school. Naturally the older children will make more intricate and technically better wind harps.

Mobiles

A mobile is a sculpture in space, characterized by movement. Alexander Calder, one of America's leading artists, has brought the mobile to a high peak in recent years so that it is now an accepted art form which is most likely to endure. The making of mobiles in schools has become very popular in recent years and a great rash of them have appeared from coast to coast. In many instances mobiles have been made without much feeling for the problems which are involved, and often they are a little more than collections of junk suspended by strings with no feeling of movement, or actual movement, or with little sensitive feeling for the materials involved.

This mobile is made of spring wire with model airplane paper glued across the looped ends. Most children will not work with this amount of care and skill.

First, to be a mobile it must move, otherwise it is like a bunch of grapes which hangs from a stem but has no motion; second, it must balance. Mobiles are not easy and may be least successful in the lower grades in the elementary school. Perhaps the fifth or sixth grade children could succeed best. To begin the mobile project it is necessary to string several pieces of wire across the room at a height at which the children can work, and to collect a good quantity of light weight materials for the making of the mobile. Thin, springy wire, fast drying airplane cement, light weight cardboard, pieces of balsa wood, light weight balls like small Christmas balls, and other similar materials are the type which will work best. Finished mobiles should give the feeling of floating or dancing gently through space; therefore, the materials should be compatible with this feeling, something which feels light and looks light. Here the use and selection of materials will help teach the children that all materials cannot do all jobs and that a sensitive selection of the materials is essential to good design. Good design in crafts results when the worker respects the limitations of the materials with which he works and when he keeps in mind the purposes to be served by the object which he is producing.

Now to make the mobile. As balance is the essential design element to be considered, each portion must be balanced. Therefore, a mobile is most easily made by working from the bottom up so that everything is in balance as you go along. The two smallest elements are balanced one against the other, perhaps on a wire, and this is hung by a silk or nylon thread. When it balances it may be attached to a wire which has a counterweight so that a perfect balance is attained at this level. This combination may be attached by means of a thread to an even larger wire which is balanced by a similar combination, perhaps only similar in weight, not in appearance; and if the placement is good, all the elements will be able to turn freely without crashing into one another. On and on it goes until the last and generally largest elements are reached at the top. The fast drying airplane cement is most useful, as pieces of cardboard or balsa wood can be easily attached with this cement to a piece of wire and will be firm in a matter of a few minutes. It is also good to put a dab of the cement any place at which a thread is attached to a wire to firmly hold the thread in place. Mobiles are fun to do but really good mobiles take good planning, just as do other craft projects. When the so-called scrap materials are treated chaotically and insensitively they remain scrap, but through a sensitive handling they can be transformed and "dematerialized" so that a bottle cap is no longer just a bottle cap but an element of design. It is important that we introduce projects of this nature as early as possible in the schools so that the children can become aware of contemporary art forms. The teacher should utilize every opportunity of this sort to develop a greater awareness of the art in the world about the children. Each craft lesson should also be a lesson in art appreciation so that the children learn to see art in everything, and not only in the galleries.

Costumes and Dressup

On most any summer's day if you watch where children play you will always find a group dressed up in old clothes and having a wonderful time improvising costumes. This desire to dress up and to play-act is generally shared by most children in the lower elementary grades. There are times when a simple costume is important to dramatize the home made play and there are times when just making costumes for the fun of making them is in order. Hats are never a problem. They can be made from paper bags or construction paper and the costumes themselves can be made from large pieces of brown wrapping paper which are folded double and an opening cut for the head, the sides can be stapled closed or sewed closed with darning needles and yarn and each child can paint or decorate his own costume in whatever manner he wishes, depending upon the circumstances. Special problems like "lets all make animals" or "lets all be princes or princesses" or "lets make party clothes" can serve as motivations and are

Most small children enjoy "dressing up" but the fun is doubled when they can make their own costumes.

Party hats present a
good exercise in
paper sculpture.

most challenging. If the community dry cleaner delivers cleaned garments in long paper bags these can be saved and used in the same manner as the folded wrapping paper, only the sides are now already closed and it is simply a matter of opening a hole for the head and arms and cutting the length to a suitable size. If the problem is cowboys or cowgirls, simple vests or just skirts for the girls may be made with paper neckerchiefs and all of them decorated with fringe or cut paper designs or painted designs. If the problem is one of spacemen then perhaps a space helmet can be made of a cardboard box with openings cut in for the face that are covered with colored cellophanes or aerials, too, might be added. Discarded clothing will make excellent play acting materials and the teacher should feel free to allow the children to cut and sew and create their own fashions from these discards.

Stuffed Paper Animals

By now the teacher is probably well aware of the values of brown wrapping paper for the craft activities of the elementary classroom. In fact, it becomes an almost indispensable material. Most small children who have had some stuffed animals to play with during their preschool years and even their early school years may enjoy making large stuffed animals from brown wrapping paper, yarn, and paint. This can be a challenging project for the small children. A large double thickness of brown wrapping paper is given to each child on which he can draw or paint a large animal or bird or fish. The teacher must pay attention to the drawings at this stage so that legs do not become too spindly or tails too thin or else when they are sewn they are too thin to be stuffed. When a good animal or bird has been painted on one piece of the paper the two thicknesses can be pinned together temporarily and the child encouraged to cut out the figure around its profile. Following this, using wads of crumpled up newspapers for stuffing, the child can begin to sew with yarn and a large needle around the edge

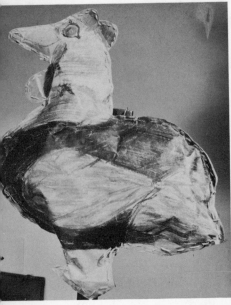

Wrapping-paper animals satisfy the need to occasionally work very large and freely. They are easily sewed with darning needles and yarn or string.

of the figure and when enough of it is thus closed, the stuffing is inserted gently to inflate the sides and this process just continues until the child has gone clear around the figure and is back to the starting point. By now the figure is fully stuffed and the other side can be painted to match the first side, or perhaps the child wants to contrast the opposite side with the first side. When the children have finished painting or crayoning these they can be hung around the room for a delightful zoo. Stuffed animals can be made on a smaller scale using cloth or oil cloth. The cloth or oil cloth can be stuffed with shredded foam rubber or with shredded nylon hose to make them soft and pleasant to handle.

Dolls

In the section called "Puppets Are a Must" a large stocking doll was described for use in puppetry. This same procedure without the puppet strings makes a lovely doll. A very simple one for the small children can be made from a man's stocking. For this you will need scissors, a needle and thread, some cotton batting for stuffing, some buttons, a piece of ribbon and maybe some bits of cloths for clothing. The toe of the stocking will make the arms. It is cut off about three inches back from the toe and then this piece is cut in half lengthwise. This makes a little triangular piece when folded double and one side of it can be closed by sewing and the triangle stuffed. Split the rest of the foot lengthwise back several inches and sew each side of the slit together to form the two legs and sew the ends closed to keep the stuffing inside. Stuff the arms and legs

Sometimes a project in doll making becomes a joint effort of parent and child. Such projects are often helpful in developing a better understanding of each other's problems.

with cotton batting. The heel becomes the seat for this is a sitting doll. Stuff it and enough more of the stocking to make the body. Tie it off with the ribbon, stuff the remaining portion for a nice round head and tie it off, and the little bit that remains can become the cap which turns down over the head. Now the arms can be sewed into place, and using additional ribbons and buttons and embroidery floss a face can be made. A piece of ribbon may make a belt, buttons may be sewed down the front and cloth may make a skirt or a scarf. Sometimes with the very youngest children these dolls can be sent home almost finished and the mother may want to help the child finish the doll or dress it for him. While we are anxious that the children learn to do their own work there are some values inherent in having the mother and child work together on the same project for a better understanding of each other.

Other simple dolls can be made just using pieces of cotton or wool or velvet. For a flat doll the child would draw his pattern on a piece of paper. Two pieces of the cloth would be placed one on top of the other on a flat surface, and the pattern which the child drew originally pinned to them and cut out around the pattern lines. This can be sewed with an over-casting stitch and the top of the head left open for stuffing. If there are features to be added these could be done more easily before stuffing. Finally a dress and hat can be made from another piece of material.

Kites

Every springtime the skies are filled with flying kites on whose strings tug small children and fathers. What fun it is to build one's own kite instead of buying one exactly like every other one in town. Kite building and kite materials are simple. Good pliable pine or bass sticks can be obtained from any lumber company; sometimes they are in the scrap box waiting and sometimes they must be cut to order. Lengths of split bamboo obtained from rug dealers may also be used. Also needed, a good quality light-weight paper such as that used in model airplane building. If kite making is a brand new experience for the teacher, she

The large flat surface of a kite is ideal for
decorating with gay and bright designs.

No other kite in town will have quite the character of this one.

should examine carefully a commercially made one in order to fully understand
the simple construction, for if kites are built they should be built to fly. Once
the principle is understood, the teacher should have no qualms about deviations,
for the class may have many children who have kite ideas they want to try out.
Some children may try two cross bars instead of the conventional one, or may
try to develop bird-like or butterfly-like ideas for their kites. Once built, the kites
should be checked to be sure that tears or loose edges are pasted down so they
will not tear in the wind. Then the kites can be painted in a fashion that the
child chooses for this project. Especially in this project, the sky's the limit.

And in Conclusion

Once a creative craft program has been used to enrich the elementary school program the teacher will need no convincing of its value. Learning becomes easier, children become happier, work habits improve, and children are always growing in their problem solving ability. The teacher knows that good materials suited to the age and interests and needs of her children are essential for an effective program, and she knows that it is necessary to plan carefully to carry out interesting and worthwhile projects and activities. It is important to develop a climate or classroom situation which permits enough freedom to encourage creative work and creative thinking. On the other hand, the teacher must exert sufficient control and provide enough direction and motivation to teach good order and good work habits. Craft work must be creative, calling upon the child to use his initiative, resourcefulness, and imagination in solving the problems presented. Each craft should provide sufficient problems to so challenge each child that at the end of the project growth has taken place. Every craft should help the aesthetic growth of the child and bring about a greater awareness of the art and beauty in the world about him. Crafts should permit the child to learn about materials, to gain respect for their limitations and yet to explore fully the possibilities of them. Crafts can make a dull world become a bright world.

Relax, enjoy yourself, and have fun in your crafts program.

tute